Challenge Management

Dr. Wladimir Klitschko is a former boxer who achieved worldwide fame as world heavyweight champion, having gained the IBF, IBO, WBO and WBA titles. Having earned a degree in Philosophy and a PhD in sports science, he is a lecturer at the University of St. Gallen as well as a successful entrepreneur.

Stefanie Bilen is a journalist and author. She has worked for magazines and newspapers such as *Handelsblatt, Harvard Business Manager* and the *Wall Street Journal*. She holds a degree in Business Studies and studied Business Journalism at the Georg-von-Holtzbrinck School for Business Journalists. She enjoys sailing and running but is yet to try boxing.

Wladimir Klitschko, Stefanie Bilen

Challenge Management

What managers can learn from the top athlete

Translated from German by Maren Barton

Campus Verlag
Frankfurt/New York

The original edition was published in 2017 by Campus Verlag with the title
Challenge Management. Was Sie als Manager vom Spitzensportler lernen können.
All rights reserved.

ISBN 978-3-593-50905-1 Print
ISBN 978-3-593-43899-3 E-Book (PDF)
ISBN 978-3-593-43900-6 E-Book (EPUB)

Cover design: Campus Verlag GmbH, Frankfurt am Main
Cover illustration: © Marc Schäfer
Typesetting: Fotosatz L. Huhn, Linsengericht
Printing: Beltz Grafische Betriebe GmbH, Bad Langensalza
Printed in Germany

www.campus.de

Content

Part I
Challenges Are the Air that We Breathe

Part II
My Twelve Ways to Respond to Challenges

Part III
How Experts Use Challenge Management Practically

Welcome

"If we make willpower an integral part of our attitude, then we can master any challenge!" That is the experience and the maxim that influenced me the most in my long-standing collaboration with Dr. Wladimir Klitschko.

It has been a great honor to work side by side with this exceptional sportsman. Every day with him allows us the chance to grow. He does not lecture; he does not instruct. Instead, he shares his know-how and his ideas with those around him as a matter of course and in a likeable, believable, and empathetic way.

With this book he is aiming to show you how a boxer's attitude can be applied to the challenges of everyday (business) life. He shares solutions that got him to where he is today: Dr. Wladimir Klitschko is one of the most respected sporting icons in the world as well as a successful businessman in charge of an international network of companies.

I hope you enjoy reading this book and wish you lots of willpower in accepting and mastering your challenges.

Tatjana Kiel
Managing Director of KLITSCHKO Ventures GmbH
t.kiel@klitschko-ventures.com

Fight, Fall, and Rise

There are some people in this world who simply are fantastic role models. They are people who are consistent and have great power of persuasion; people who are persistent and become successful because of this.

This is the kind of person I consider Wladimir Klitschko to be. I have to say I am very proud to know him. This is a man who is characterized by a big heart, extraordinary passion, and strong integrity. He is also a wonderful friend.

In our lives so far there have been a number of similarities that connect us.

We are both modest and know our roots. Both our lives were strongly shaped by our parents. He grew up in the former Soviet Union, whereas I lived in the working-class town of Amityville in New York State.

Both of us are hungry for success. Already during our teenage years we knew that we wanted more from life. Wladimir was demonstrating his talent in the boxing ring early on in Ukraine. I was working three part-time jobs in parallel in order to be able eventually to buy my own small shop in Amityville. That was the beginning of my career as an entrepreneur.

We both owe our success to particular values that matter to us. Wladimir's persistence, flexibility, focus, and coordination have always been an inspiration to me. I have always been convinced that trust is the most important asset for us as humans. Especially in times like these the world needs more empathy, more trust and more love.

Lastly, we are also connected by our view that real leaders are characterized by what they give to the world and not by what is given to them.

In this sense, let me tell you about myself and introduce you to this fascinating book by Wladimir, in which he shares his worldview with us.

I remember my childhood in Long Island in New York State. The people I knew were honest, hard-working people. I delivered newspapers, packed bags at grocery shops, and worked as a waiter. I learnt a lot. Some things I learnt fast, others more slowly.

One night our family was standing in the street. We could only watch helplessly as our house was burning down. I was still small, so there would have been no shame in it if I had been scared or upset about our loss. But at that moment my mother gave me a piece of her wisdom that I often think about: "Bill, there is nothing in that house that is more important than what is out here."

Moments like that laid the foundation for my life-long optimism. I internalized that no-one and nothing can take away a person's dreams. No matter what happens. I learnt that it is dreams that are the hallmark of a winner.

Decades later—after all my youthful dreams had come true and I had built a successful career—I was taking part in a book club event in Walldorf in Germany. During the conversation a colleague got up and said something that humbled me:

"Bill, I read your autobiography Winners Dream. *The advice your mother gave you impressed me very much: 'The best thing about you is you.' I pinned this quote to my fridge and show it to my children every day. It really means a lot to us all. Many, many thanks.*"

Her words moved me deeply. This colleague reminded me that a person who is aware of their uniqueness cannot be stopped by anyone—not by competitors or by obstacles.

She also made me aware that in our lives there are more things that unite us than that separate us. We all have one dream in life. We know how closely the scope of the dream, our imagination and our courage are linked to how much we actually achieve.

We have all forged our own paths, were often successful, yet we frequently failed, too. Because no dream becomes a reality if we don't keep an eye on the details and their significance for the whole.

The world is full of surprises, as we know all too well. And nothing changes our way of thinking faster than the awareness that our world is constantly changing and that nothing stays as it was.

Yet there is something that distinguishes the individual from the masses.

How do we get through a tough fight? What drives us to get up again after we fall? How do we create a balance between our mind and our unyielding will? My experiences have taught me that this is the toughest test of all.

It feels as if it was yesterday: It was a perfectly normal summer's day and we were celebrating my father's birthday. My brother was there; we played golf and then enjoyed a cozy dinner at his home. It was a perfect day. I remember how glad I was about this time spent with my family because in this globalized and digitalized world these moments with our loved ones unfortunately are becoming few and far between.

During the night I left the guest room at my brother's house to refill my water glass. It was dark and I slipped on the stairs; the glass broke and I fell into the shards. My face was severely injured, especially my left eye. It was one of those crazy accidents that we think only ever happen to others.

In the moments after my fall I could feel two forces fight for control over my behavior: mind versus will.

I realized that the mind was trying to evade the pain.

My mind was therefore telling me: "It's okay. Just lie here. Go to sleep. Because if you stand up, everything will get a whole lot harder." Very rational.

Yet, although the mind controls us almost completely, it does not manage to break our will.

It was my will that gave me clarity. "You have the most wonderful family, the greatest colleagues and friends in the world. They are all counting on you. Now get up and carry on!" I was badly injured and knew that getting better was going to take a long time. And yet, I pulled myself up that night. I obeyed my will. Some of the best medical experts in the world started looking after me and I got the best care imaginable. My wife Julie, my family, my friends and colleagues were always at my side, which was a real blessing.

I especially remember Hasso Plattner, the co-founder and chairman of the supervisory board of my company, SAP. He told me: "Bill, you always think about how you can support others. Now it's our turn to help you. Whatever you need, you can count on us."

I was fighting for my health and gave it everything I had as anyone would. Unfortunately, however, my left eye was beyond saving. Nonetheless, I had the feeling that I could see more than before. I had become aware that seeing is more than just observing with our eyes. It is also about what we feel and what emotions we create in others. This creates totally new forces.

I know now that this fight between mind and will not only shapes our character but actually reveals it. It is in moments like these that the full force of our personal life experiences breaks through to the surface and makes us scream our passion. It is our will that makes us get up, start running and carry on. Winners always get up and winners rise!

Wladimir is one of the greatest boxing champions in history. But that is not what is special about him, nor is it the driving force behind his ascent. At the bottom of his heart he is and always will be a challenger.

A champion receives trophies and honors—usually well deserved. But a challenger invests every last fiber of his heart and his soul.

In this book we find out in person from the ultimate challenger how we can master the challenges life throws at us. Or as he likes to put it: "If you know how to control your mind, then you can control anything."

We all fight. We all fall. And we all have within us the ability to get up again and to rise.

In Wladimir we have a role model that we can trust.

Bill McDermott
SAP SE CEO and Executive Board Member
March 2017

What a Fight!

"Failure is not an option!" This is a conviction I have held since my first defeat. For me as a professional athlete there has only been one option ever since: to get in the ring to win. Otherwise there would be no point in taking part, even less in taking on an opponent.

When I lost against Tyson Fury in the winter of 2015 after years of successes and with the arrangements for the rematch dragging on, a new dimension developed. My main objective in the preparations was no longer just to preclude a defeat in the next fight. Instead, I wanted that victory with my whole heart and everything else got subordinated to that goal. That Fury cancelled the rematch in the end and that in Anthony Joshua I found an opponent who offered me the greatest stage of all as well as the greatest of all challenges, just strengthened this conviction. After all, a professional boxer does not often get the chance to fight against the best of the best, despite a previous defeat, in front of 90,000 spectators in a fight televised in more than 150 countries. I was obsessed with the idea of winning. Anything I and my team were doing from then on, we were doing obsessively.

Obsession—isn't it strange that this term has negative connotations? If people talk about obsession, they mean stubbornness and even a bit of madness and delusion. Yet I see this term as entirely positive. In my understanding obsession means one thing and one thing only: complete and unconditional love.

My aim was to win the fight against 27-year-old Anthony Joshua on 29 April 2017. I was obsessed with this idea and 100 per cent convinced that I was going to reach this goal. Despite my conviction that I was going to win, the result of the fight showed that I had lost the competition. Yet in the ring I succeeded in getting back up several times after being knocked down and I even managed to knock my opponent to the ground. It may sound strange: I didn't win the fight, but left the ring a winner nonetheless. I had triumphed over my biggest enemy: myself.

The feedback I got after this fight was overwhelming. Reporters were united in saying that I had fought with my heart and my brains and had demonstrated greatness despite being defeated. "Wladimir Klitschko has shown that even as a loser you can leave the ring a hero", one of the commentators said. My number of fans increased and the positivity and encouragement from all over the world was huge.

If I had defeated Anthony Joshua in the first round, this would surely have been different. There seems to be truth in what one journalist wrote: "Klitschko appeared greater in his defeat than he ever managed in his victories."

As a consequence I have reconsidered my guiding principle because now I know: "Failure is an option"—and in this case a very good option. I did not achieve my goal of winning the fight, but I did reach another, much bigger goal: worldwide recognition and respect, for me as well as for boxing as a sport. By "failing" I achieved a much greater success than I would have done by winning.

However, being obsessive remains important to me. I have to love what I am doing. I have to be able to give it my everything. One can lose a fight, but one cannot lose an obsession.

Since 29 April 2017 I have come to see: Success does not necessarily mean reaching a predetermined goal. Rather, it means achieving the best possible result—and sometimes we just cannot even envisage beforehand what result might be the best one possible.

Following that night I redefined the meaning of being successful.

Failure with obsession—that is an option!

Yours, *W. Klitschko*   30th April 2017

Part I

Challenges Are the Air that We Breathe

1. How It All Began

The man was twice my height. At least. I was standing in front of him with my head tipped back to look up at him, and my mother was standing a little behind me. I was incredibly proud and quite excited. The head teacher of the elementary school had taken the time to meet me because there was something I needed to talk to him about. It was about my future.

I was six years old and fed up with being in kindergarten. I was supposed to go to school aged seven as was normal in the USSR, but I did not want to wait that long. I had been going to kindergarten for years; my mother was working there teaching the preschool class. Every morning we walked there together. I played the same games, met the same children, sang similar songs year after year. I had had enough and wanted something new. Time and again I had complained to my mother and every time she said the same thing: "All children only go to school when they are seven. There are no exceptions and all the top classes are full."

Eventually, when I was moaning at her again—and I was very persistent in my nagging, almost mind-numbingly so, as my mother assured me later on—she had had enough: "If you really are so determined and you definitely want to go, then you have to prove it", she told me. "We are going to go to the head teacher and then you can ask him yourself."

If my mother had hoped that her announcement would frighten me and deter me from my wish, she was wrong. I was jubilant. I was still only a little boy, yet my fighting spirit had been awakened. I wanted to be allowed to go to school as soon as possible and become one of the big boys. I imagined how wonderful it would be to be taken seriously: to be able to learn important things and be given tasks. I visualized myself sitting in my classroom on my own chair and at a proper desk, a bigger one than the kindergarten ones.

My mother made an appointment and thus I was now standing in front of an old gentleman to ask him to make an exception to the rule. "You do know that all children are only allowed to go to school aged seven, don't you?", he asked me. I nodded and replied that I was not afraid of the older children. After all Vitali, my brother, was five years older than me. "Do you also know that we have a totally different program here than in kindergarten?", he continued. "Here children have to complete tasks and do what the teachers tell them". "I know", I answered joyfully. "Are you prepared to follow these rules?", he asked. I nodded eagerly. That was exactly what I wanted.

The head teacher exchanged looks with my mother and then talked to her in hushed tones for a while. Eventually he bent down to me and shook my hand. "Wladimir, in that case you will go to school aged six. I hope you won't disappoint us", he said earnestly. "I have to admit that I have never had a six-year-old stand in front of me with such courage and such a strong will and argue his wish so self-confidently."

I was happy. I threw my arms around my mother's neck and at home I told my father and my grandmother that I was going to school soon. I felt content and incredibly satisfied. I had accomplished my dream. The next few years were going to show my family and the teachers that it had been the right decision.

Back then I did not think much about it, but I had learnt something: No matter how old or young I was—it is always worthwhile fighting for goals that matter, irrespective of the obstacles along the way. The most important thing is that I believe in myself, persist and do not give up.

As I found out later, this was a pattern that repeated itself throughout my childhood and youth: If I got an idea in my head I turned to my mother. She was the person I talked to about my plans, my desires and visions. She never just put them into action for me, though, nor did she give me the solutions on a silver platter. Instead, she helped me find my own way. That is how I learnt to champion my wishes and push them through. When I was still a child this required me to be sure of what I wanted and to argue it well in order to reach my goals.

This was especially necessary to stand my ground against my older brother Vitali. It was not just him who thought he was superior to me; my mother shared this view of us. "Vova", she often told me, "there are those who lead and those who are being led. Your brother Vitali belongs in the first group, you probably more in the second."

How I hated it when she said that! Yes, my brother is five years older than me and my parents had given him the responsibility for me. As they both worked, it was often my brother who looked after me or who I went along with. But did that by necessity mean that he had to be the leader—and I his subordinate? After all, I was just as courageous and determined as he was.

Possibly this is the reason why I persistently got on my mother's nerves with a view to winning her over to my plans when I was still a young boy. I was lucky that she realized that I was the kind of child who needed to be stimulated and challenged; a child who needed to be given tasks and challenges to thrive and develop. She usually indulged my demands, but without making it too easy for me. She wanted to make sure that I really wanted it.

I remember another story: I was eleven at the time and it was just before the long summer vacation. I had three months without school ahead of me. My mother told me that there was a vacation job going at her company. We were by then living in Kiev and my mother was working at a company that manufactured elevators. I wanted to earn some extra pocket money and enthusiastically said yes.

On my first day at work I became the proud owner of a grey company overall, which was going to be my uniform for the next few months. My responsibilities were clearly outlined: sweeping the grounds, painting the curbs white, and disassembling the electrical contacts of malfunctioning elevators.

That the work was boring did not concern me. I was glad to have secured this job. There was work that needed to be done, and I was getting paid for it. Consequently, every morning I looked forward to what lay ahead and went about my work dutifully day after day.

When I got my first wages after a month, my mother wanted to collect them for me. But I was much too proud of it to let her do it. I queued up for my pay with all the other workers and felt incredibly grown up. My first hard-earned wages!

What I did not know at the time was that I did not have an official job and therefore there were no wages. My mother had invented the vacation job for me and had let her colleagues in on the secret, including the lady at the pay office. She wanted me to have something worthwhile to do during the holidays and for me to learn that if I wanted money I had to earn it. It was her way of having trust in my abilities and strengthening my self-confidence.

Her plan ran into trouble when another boy also started doing a holiday job. His name was Andrey and he was given the same tasks as me: sweeping, painting, unscrewing. The unfair thing about it was that he was paid 50 kopeks an hour, but I only got 25. I could not get my head around that and tried talking to my mum about it. The fact that I was supposed to show him the ropes, that he was unreliable and did not even turn up for work every day, just made matters worse.

My mother just shrugged. She should have come to an agreement with Andrey's mother beforehand. His holiday job, of course, had also just been made up by his mum, but she could not tell me that back then. There was nothing I could do but put up with the difference in pay.

By the end of the holidays I had earned 10 rubles. I used that money to fulfill a long-held wish and bought myself some white summer shoes. The warm part of the year was almost over, but I did not care. It was the first money I had earned myself and I had spent exhausting, monotonous weeks saving it up. I wore the shoes with pride and dignity—even in autumn.

Discipline and a sense of duty were virtues that had been instilled in my brother and me from the moment we were born. Just like honesty and respect. All of our male ancestors had been soldiers in the army and our father was living these values at all times and insisting that we did, too.

If a task was assigned to us, then it was to be done and to be reported back on. It did not matter whether this took days, weeks or months, whether we wanted to or not. That was not what it was about and we were taught this from the start. Nonetheless, that did not mean I never tried to test the limits and to disregard the values for a little while from time to time.

When I was ten, I was searching for a regular leisure-time activity. My brother Vitali was 15 and had already started kickboxing training.

At my age that was not yet an option. So my mother asked me: "What would you like to do?" On TV I had stolen a quick—forbidden—glance at breakdancing and had been fascinated by those young Americans throwing themselves to the ground in such cool and casual ways, just to spin around and jump up again in time to the music.

I discovered that at the other end of Kiev there was a breakdancing school and told my mother that I would like to take lessons there. Unfortunately at five rubles per month the course was very expensive and we would not have been able to afford it easily. Yet I had set my mind on it and kept pestering my mother. To my surprise she gave in after a while.

On the first day of the course she handed me the money and admonished me not to lose it under any circumstances. She trusted me to find my way across town and get there safely. After all I was often out by myself. I wanted to save myself the bus fare, as I frequently did, and walked there that afternoon. I hurried along without paying attention to what was to my left or right until a slot machine on the wall of a building caught my attention. I stopped, magically attracted by the game. Even now I cannot explain where this sudden, previously totally unknown fascination came from. I was watching the twinkling lights and imagined a pile of coins falling clinkingly into the coin tray. Suddenly I was captivated by the idea of adding to my money. I just needed to win once or twice and with luck I would be able to multiply my money. On the spur of the moment I asked for change. Coin after coin landed in the games machine. Yet, unfortunately I did not win either in the first or indeed any of the following rounds. In the end I only stopped when I had lost all my money. The fortune I had hoped for had not come my way. I realized that for the next four weeks I had no money left to learn how to breakdance. I had gambled it all away.

A guilty conscience hit me, and I waited for two hours before I dared to go home. My family asked me excitedly how I had liked the lesson and wanted to see first steps and moves. I made excuses and did not dare admit to my mistake. The trust my mother had placed in me was too imposing, the amount of money I had pointlessly wasted too large. Therefore I left my father, my grandmother, my brother and my mother with their belief that I had actually completed my first training session.

And so it carried on: Week after week I left the house supposedly to go breakdancing and in between I practiced the moves, turns and steps I had seen on TV in front of the mirror. This continued for twelve weeks because I spent the next two months' fees on gambling, too. Nonetheless, I got really very good at breakdancing. My family cheered every time I showed them the moves I had taught myself, and even now my mother still does not know the truth about this, I think. For a long time I could not decide which feeling I should give the upper hand to: my worry about getting caught after all and getting into trouble or my joy at having made the best of my mistake and having taught myself how to breakdance.

Now I know: My childhood and youth were characterized by tasks that exceeded those usually expected of schoolchildren, as well as by strong discipline. Because of my family's frequent moves—as a high-ranking officer in the army, my father was transferred to different locations every few years—my brother and I had to get used to new classes, teachers and environments time and again. If school and homework did not challenge me sufficiently, my mother provided other tasks. She constantly gave me novels to read in order to make me think. If I did not have anything to do during the vacations, she found me jobs. To stop me from getting bored she had me help with the housework or enabled me to try out new hobbies. And if all of that was not enough I went looking for my own adventures.

I created my own tasks for myself, including small thrills and dares.

As a consequence of all this, I did not think it at all unusual to go to boarding school at age 14. My brother had done the same a few years earlier. I was ready to leave home and take my life largely into my own hands because I had a goal: I wanted to travel and get to know the world.

In the Soviet Union all young people leave general education after eight years and then their paths split into going to vocational school, middle school or boarding school, normally at the age of 15. However, because I had started earlier than was usual, I was only 14 when I had to make this decision about my future career.

For my father the choice was obvious: Like him and all of his male ancestors I was to go to a military school. He chose the Suvorov School for me, a cadet school dating back to the 18th century that had always had the reputation of providing both an outstanding military and general education.

My mother, however, saw further abilities and strengths in me. She suggested that I might want to consider becoming a doctor and I liked that idea. So as not to disappoint my father I decided to become a military doctor. I applied to the medical technical school. My good grades ensured I was invited to sit the entrance exam—even for my preferred specialization as an otorhinolaryngologist. My results were good and I was offered a place. However, because I was a year younger than all the other applicants, I was not allowed to start immediately. A nice lady at the admissions office told me I should spend the next twelve months training as a nurse to bridge the gap.

I could not believe my ears! My dream was to become a doctor, and that as quickly as possible. Doing nursing was unimaginable to me, so I thanked her and left.

Then I had to hurry because the window for applications for most schools was going to end just a few days later. With hindsight that time pressure was helpful in making me make the right decision. I decided against the military school my father had recommended and instead applied to a school that specialized in sports.

Vitali's example had opened my eyed to the chances boxing was offering him. What could be more obvious than to follow his example, as he was my role model, closest companion and best friend? He was by then studying sports science at university and had been taking part in international kickboxing and boxing competitions for years. A few months earlier he had been to the USA. This may sound funny, but I had been deeply impressed: He had brought back Coca-Cola, American t-shirts and other souvenirs from the US. I wanted a slice of that, too!

Boxing was to be the means to this aim. Sport was to enable me to fulfill my dream of going traveling. That is why I intuitively, within a very short time, decided to go to the sports boarding school.

My parents reacted cautiously when I told them, but they supported me nonetheless. After all, my father knew that sports require a lot of discipline and this appealed to him. Both my parents agreed to me going there. I applied and was granted a place to specialize in boxing for the next two years, just as I had wished.

It was hard to begin with. The journey from school to my home took a few hours, which meant I could only go home on the weekends, if that. In the beginning I was terribly homesick. Boarding school life was very different to how I had imagined it. I had to share a room with five other boys; our days were strictly structured from the moment we got up to the moment we went to bed: two hours of school in the morning, boxing training, two hours of school, lunch, two hours of school, boxing training, dinner. In between all that I had to do my laundry, too, which left little time for any other activities.

At least our commitment reaped its rewards. We were quickly entered for boxing competitions. Those of us who did well soon travelled right across the Soviet Union and a little later even as far as the other Eastern Bloc countries and Germany. This was such a privilege! To leave the country, get to know other nations and cultures and especially to be allowed to see the West was something that only a very select few were allowed in the Soviet Union: politicians and sportspeople.

In order to achieve this, I quickly realized, I had to perform at an accordingly high level. In the beginning I was on the receiving end of the punches. My first proper fight took place at my sports school and I was quite overwhelmed. I did not manage to apply what I had learnt in training when I was in the boxing ring for real, and I did not dare throw a proper punch. I stood no chance and was utterly out of my depth in that situation. The result showed itself very visibly over the next few days: My face was black and blue and I even sported some cuts. Looking in the mirror I didn't recognize myself and I was physically hurting all over my body.

It was lucky that I had always been a quick learner and I decided I could not let this happen again.

Yet my second fight did not go much better, especially as it had the added excitement of being my first 'away' fight. It took place in a circus in Belarus, and the tent was full to bursting. My knees were shaking just from the sheer number of spectators. To begin with I landed a few hits, but after that I froze. I got beaten again big time until the referee stopped the fight because I was showing no activity. The pressure was just too much: the audience, the atmosphere, the opponent, the referee—it all intimidated me. The situation was not at all comparable to the training. I realized that being good in the training room does not mean winning the fight. I had to be not just fit physically but also strong mentally. Many athletes win not through their muscles but in their head.

My face looked awful again for the next few days. And yet, I never once questioned whether I had chosen the wrong sport. I just had to get better at it and find a way to display the same desire to win in the boxing ring that I already had in training.

So far, my desire to travel the world had been the deciding factor; this was my aim; this was why I had chosen to go to the sports school. However, if I carried on like I had started, I would very quickly have to write off this dream of seeing the big wide world. I needed to succeed, as I could see from Vitali's example. The only reason why he was getting ahead was that he won his fights and dominated his opponents. Interestingly, his motive was very different to mine: He had a burning passion for his sport and to him the traveling was something that came with it. He was a born fighter, and that is how boxing became his gateway to the world.

All of this became clear to me after my first two fights. I had to work harder and really want to beat my opponent. Destroy him.

Because it was always one or the other of the two athletes in the ring who got beaten up; myself or the other guy. On occasion both got beaten up, but whoever was mentally stronger was the person who left the ring as winner.

I did not ever want to be guy again who looked a wreck after the fight, so therefore I had to become more courageous and more active and I needed to demonstrate more will to win. I had to get out of my comfort zone, and pronto! I started playing through my fights in my mind, preparing myself for the opponent, and visualizing myself leaving the ring as the winner.

This mental preparation already helped me in my next fight. In my mind's eye I could see my battered face and I remembered the pain. These two memories helped me to shed my shyness and attack. It's him or me, that was what I was constantly aware of thereafter. Sure enough I won my third fight and all subsequent ones. I had understood that it was both about physical fitness and mental strength. From then on, I did anything I could to prepare myself holistically for my opponents, with my mind and my body.

This reaped rewards for me in many ways. Being successful meant that I suffered only minor injuries and even started earning money through my sport. I was 15 years old when in the Ukrainian city of Donetsk I won my first competition that carried prize money: 100 US dollars. I could not believe my luck! So much money! At that time my parents earned the equivalent of 10 US dollars per month—in the shape of food vouchers.

I used some of the money to get a gift for my brother, seat covers for his car, a Lada that he had saved up for and bought from his own cash prizes.

From then on we were having a whale of a time. We thought we were on top of the world. We were allowed to travel, enjoyed sporting successes and earned the respect of our friends and relatives, who admiringly started calling us "The Champs".

Of course, not everyone understood the path that we were taking from then on. The US heavyweight boxer and former world champion Lamon Brewster even now cannot understand our career and our role in the sport: "Those who decide to take up boxing usually have no other choice", he once said in an interview. This is because boxers are often from the lower social classes and drop out of school early, and few manage to complete job training. The fact that both Vitali and I gained university degrees and yet decided to take up boxing is something that Lamon Brewster considered absurd: "The Klitschkos had the whole wide world open to them. They could have become lawyers or doctors. So why did they choose boxing?"

Brewster probably saw only half the picture, however. He grew up in the United States of America, so at least theoretically the whole world had always been open to him anyway. This was not the case for Vitali and me. We inhabited a small socialist microcosm from which we could see very few ways of breaking free. Only through sport did our world open up. In addition, we appreciated boxing for being one of the oldest and most honorable sports. Without our sporting success we would never have got that far.

And I would never have won the Olympic Games.

The path I chose led me from the sports boarding school to university, while my main interest was still boxing. In spring 1993 I became Junior European Heavyweight Champion in Greece. At age 20 I moved to Germany in order to compete for BC Flensburg in the German premier league (1. Bundesliga), and when I was 20 I came second at the European Championships in Denmark. This success then paved the way to my ultimate goal: the Olympic Games in Atlanta in 1996.

For years I had been dreaming of an Olympic medal. No boxer from the former Soviet Union had ever won an Olympic gold medal in the heavyweight division. I wanted to be the first one to achieve this! I wanted to become an Olympic Champion.

I trained like a man obsessed despite the preparations being extremely arduous. I got food poisoning and for months suffered from high blood pressure that the doctors just could not find a cause for. When I was allowed to carry the Ukrainian flag on Maidan Square before I flew out to Atlanta, I was so proud. Considering my physical condition, however, I did not really think I stood a chance of winning that gold medal. My inner voice was telling me: "Be glad that you qualified. Let's wait and see what the chances are for any medal."

Despite all previous difficulties I did in fact win the first bout. After that I secured at least bronze, and then silver. "Be proud of yourself", my inner voice told me again, and then it added: "Keep going, there's more that's possible."

My opponent in the fight for the gold medal was especially strong. Even just in physical terms, at 150 kg Paea Wolfgramm, a boxer from Tonga, was superior to me. In the night before the fight I dreamed that I was going to lose against him. Not a good omen as up until then what I had dreamed the night before a bout had always come true.

It looked like this was going to be the case this time, too. I was behind in round one. "Stupid dream", I thought grumpily. Yet I did not want to give up so close to the goal. "Not under any circumstances will I give up", I encouraged myself. I was proud of what I had achieved, but I wanted more: "Just forget about that dream; I want to win." In the end I won on points. My biggest wish had come true despite some challenges to me and my abilities: a gold medal at the Olympic Games.

I could hardly believe my luck. This medal was the start of my career as a professional boxer, it opened a lot of doors and afforded me new possibilities. It quickly became clear, however, that this new satisfaction was not going to last long. I wanted more! I needed a new goal and a new challenge:

The title of World Champion.

I really cannot say that I was feeling bored at the time. I had had an intense year with 15 fights at BC Flensburg in the German Bundesliga followed by the preparation for the Olympic Games. Then I, together with Vitali, started with a boxing promoter in Hamburg, doing 15 or 16 bouts per year. I was either training for a fight or had just finished one. In addition, there were marketing appearances and sponsoring duties. Besides all of that, I was also writing my doctoral thesis in Sports Sciences.

Despite all the above, I needed a new sporting motivation; something big; something never seen before. On the one hand, I never knew back then who my next opponent was going to be, who I was going to meet when and in what condition. I myself could be injured or fall ill. There were many variables that I had no influence on. On the other hand, it appealed to me to set myself high aims rather than just to think about the next step in my career.

It became increasingly obvious to me that I needed big challenges to motivate myself and to keep stretching myself and developing further.

If anything gets in the way then these obstacles just spur me on even more to stick to my goals. While some people consider it megalomania or restlessness, this is what I need like the air that I breathe: one challenge after the other.

I am convinced that this way of life makes many of us happier and more successful human beings. It is satisfying to strive for something; to leave one's comfort zone; to set new, higher goals and to reach them; to deal with obstacles and to consciously inhabit one's success. Obviously not everyone can become world champion, but my approach works on a smaller scale, too.

I experienced this a while ago when I was traveling with my nephew. We were spending an August weekend at the seaside in Southern France. Max, my brother Vitali's son, is a surprisingly good swimmer despite being only eight years old. We were on a long snorkeling tour. When I wanted to swim into a cave with him, he stopped. The dark opening seemed to look uninviting to him. Even worse, it was windy, the sea was a little rough, rocks were blocking the view. "I'm afraid," Max said and wanted to swim past the cave. "Afraid of what?" I asked him. "We are only afraid of what we do not know. If we swim into the cave and have a look, I'm sure we will see that there's nothing to be afraid of." I knew that place because I had swum there a few times before. It was a harmless cave in the rocks.

Max was paddling on the spot with his flippers. He was clearly in two minds: He was clearly daunted by the darkness, but I could also see that he wanted to prove himself—to himself and, I'm sure, also to me. He turned to me, noticed the trust in my look and pulled himself together. Slowly, close together, we swam into the rocky cave.

What I knew from my previous swims was confirmed: There was nothing unusual to see in the cave. And that was exactly as intended: I had wanted to show Max that it is good consciously to find things out and that it is important to understand one's fears, to accept them and then to overcome them. I was very proud of him for taking me up on the challenge, and I could see that he was pleased with himself, too: "It is great that you dared do that. And you know what? When we're here next you are going to swim into that cave without any hesitation because there is nothing unknown in there any more now. If you hadn't conquered your fear, then you would always keep avoiding the cave. And you wouldn't even know what you might be missing."

The boy beamed and I was delighted to the bottom of my heart. It had seemed to be such a small everyday occurrence, but it had made him grow. He had understood that we should not run away from things that appear daunting. If we recognize the challenge, accept it and master it, we win twofold: not just by understanding that the fear was actually baseless, but also that we become more courageous once we have overcome it.

And I had learnt something too: that just as I myself need challenges, I also like challenging others.

Summary

- Boxing enabled me to fulfill my dream: to travel.
- I learnt early on that it is worth fighting for my goals.

- Discipline and a sense of duty helped me on my way.
- Physical fitness and mental strength are the prerequisites for sustainable success.
- Obstacles spur me on to reach my goal.

2. Ergo sum: I Know Who I Am

I owe so much to boxing, and yet I fell into it by chance rather than design. It was Vitali who decided he wanted to take up kick boxing and later on classic boxing. That was the impetus that set the course for me—being five years his junior—to follow in his tracks.

For as long as I can remember I have always looked to my brother for guidance. Our parents had given him the responsibility of taking care of me early on. I accompanied him everywhere. He was my childminder, my leader, my role model. He was also my best friend.

If he was interested in sports, I was interested. If he went to training, I went along. If he got into the ring, I was feverishly looking forward to my first fight.

It did not matter to me at all that we were five years apart in age. Quite the opposite: I learnt from his experiences. I watched him and absorbed whatever he said. "If he can learn this, then I can too," I convinced myself. In my mind, there were no limits. Yet, I realized at some point that Vitali was a born "fighter", his innate ability was a natural gift. A similar ability was slumbering within me that many people around me called talent. However, I had to unearth it first, which took a lot of hard work helped by a significant amount of ambition. Later on, we came up with catchy motivational slogans: "Born to fight," I coined for Vitali. "Born to win," he took to calling out to me.

I wanted to be one of the best, wanted to be promoted to the league in which Vitali had already made a name for himself. Ideally, I would have liked to get better even than my brother because if I could manage to do that then I would be able to defeat anyone.

As long as I was physically smaller than my brother, this ambition was hopeless. Nonetheless, we spurred each other on, motivated and supported each other. This continued even when we started boxing in the same weight class. We trained with rather than against each other and never saw the other as an opponent. We could never have imagined an official bout against each other and no prize in the world would have persuaded us to enter a fight against the other one, even more so as we had promised this to our mother and we respected our family.

It is mainly thanks to our parents that our success did not go to our heads. Our father had instilled within us not just discipline and stamina but also roots and respect. My mother, being a teacher, had made sure that we saw education as the most important tool to set us up for life.

Therefore, it was an obvious choice for both of us to finish university despite training in our sports, and even to continue and gain a PhD. Our parents would likely not have accepted anything less. Their conviction that they communicated to us was that we needed education in order to be able to earn a living. There were no professional sportspeople in the Soviet Union and therefore this did not count as a job. In addition, education was highly valued and sought after wherever it was available. This was a conviction that I never questioned.

When I did actually become a professional athlete at age 20, it seemed natural to me to carry on working on my PhD thesis. The topic was "Pedagogic Control in Sports Regarding Children and Young People between 14 and 19 Years of Age," and I was very interested in it as it linked into my own experience.

Some of my friends from boarding school had ended their sporting career before it had really begun because they could not stand the physical and psychological pressures. This led me to do research at my old school over several years, during which time just under 70 pupils were subjected to performance tests. I then compared their results with a view to why some failed while others performed better than normal. My theories about this formed the center of my dissertation.

My father was pleased that I took the time for my academic studies besides my bouts and training. "Boxing is not a job," he commented frequently during our youth when we were rejoicing in our competition victories.

In a certain sense he was right about this: As with any other sport, a career in boxing is a time-limited profession. At some point all athletes have to decide what the right moment is to leave the professional stage. In the best case, this happens before the athlete is forced to retire by a series of defeats or by his own body. It is clear to everyone that this retirement from sport comes long before other workers' normal pensionable age.

I am glad that even while I was still active in my sport I already established other legs to stand on professionally: as an entrepreneur, a lecturer, a founder, to name just a few.

I was able to do all of this because of my sporting successes. Boxing, as I understood right from the start, is a tool to me; a means to an end. It is not fulfillment, and it definitely is not the final destination or the end of the line. It has always provided me with the possibility to accomplish my dreams and to develop further.

In retrospect, if I consider my successes as well as my defeats in boxing and beyond, then I can identify seven themes that have determined my actions. In the beginning I used my gut feeling to apply these elements like a filter. It is not by coincidence that they reflect my philosophy and my way of making decisions over the past thirty years.

It became increasingly important to me that the people who worked with me in my companies understood these motives. That is why we identified, summarized and documented them. These days this is what the management in my companies and ventures use as a filter to make decisions independently while ensuring that these decisions are in line with what I would have done. It is the central theme that guides us when we found new business divisions or develop new products and services.

"ERGO SUM" (Latin for "Therefore I Am") stands for these seven elements that form the foundation of my philosophy. It is an abbreviation in which each letter of the two words represents one element. At the same time the phrase as a whole expresses my way of looking at life: "Ergo sum"—therefore I am. To me it is clear who I am.

Some might think this is a trite old phrase. Yet "Ergo sum" really does run through my life like a central thread:

E – Expertise (based on my experience and on science)

R – Rightness (developed according to my ethical guidelines)

G – Globalism (360 degrees, without limits, international)

O – Optimism (always thinking positively and with vision)

S – Sustainability (taking the long-term view and being environmentally conscious)

U – Uncomplexity (easy to explain and easy to understand)

M – Maximum (always striving to achieve the best and the optimum)

E—Expertise
Expertise Based on My Experience and on Science

"Knowledge and experiences become more valuable if they are shared."

Everyone has and needs expertise in order to build their business or do their job well, that is for sure. To me, the term has an additional dimension. I have been a professional athlete for more than 20 years and have accumulated a lot of knowledge and experience not just regarding boxing but also related spheres. This knowledge and experience I pass on in everything I do: to sportspeople and especially to managers, advisers and entrepreneurs; even to children and youths.

It took me a while to realize that in decades of activity I had accumulated a lot more knowledge than during my time at university and during my PhD. I had always called this undefined wealth of experience my gut feeling, but it was much more. I had long since internalized the key to success. If I have the will to struggle through and never give up; if I find a new path to my goal when stuck and then follow this path determinedly; if I take charge of my life and trust other people's expertise in certain areas, then I will be rewarded in the end.

2003 was the first time I very consciously counted on my expertise. At that time there was hardly anything else I could have built on.

This is what happened: I was fighting against Corrie Sanders in Hannover. Over the years I had got used to winning and had defended my title of world champion five times through knockout victories. But then I lost against the South African Sanders. The bout was over after only two rounds, very abruptly and totally unexpectedly. I was stunned. No-one, least of all me, had expected this. People had started calling me Dr. Steelhammer by then because of the effectiveness of my jabs—meaning the fast straight punches with my left hand. The press was unanimously saying that I was in the best phase of my career. I myself felt physically fit and was sure to win. And then the defeat. It felt as if my ego had been crushed by a steamroller.

A year later I got the chance to win back the title of world champion. I had won the necessary qualifying fights and was going to meet the US athlete Lamon Brewster in Las Vegas. As always I had prepared well for it. The fight was going well and in the beginning I dominated clearly and even floored my opponent once. But then the tide turned. In the end Brewster left the ring the winner and I was taken to hospital with a suspected brain hemorrhage. The situation was critical. My brother Vitali, who had been watching the fight, was beside himself with worry. Fortunately I was already able to be discharged the following morning. The initial diagnosis had proved to be wrong. Physically I was fit again soon after. Mentally, however, I was shattered.

The consequences of this defeat were dramatic. "Well, that was that with your boxing," Vitali said to me. Two clear defeats—to him that was a glaring sign that I ought to stop and end my career. I was shocked. He wanted to write me off this quickly? Again and again he talked to me, told me he worried about me and advised me to hang up my boxing gloves once and for all. This carried on for weeks and months. Even at the training camp before my next bout he criticized me loud and clear. He kept interfering with my training. Eventually I exploded and we had a terrible argument. It nearly turned into a brawl and in the end I threw him out. It was the first time we had a proper, heated quarrel and it ended with me banning him from entering the training camp.

This was not easy for me and very hard for Vitali. No-one likes being put in their place rudely by their little brother. However, I had no other options. My back was to the wall. I was ready to make difficult choices.

It was not just Vitali who wrote me off at that time. When I just about won my next fight, the German TV channel Premiere, which had only just signed me, dropped me again. They were not interested in broadcasting another one of my fights. Not long before, we had been portrayed in the renowned US magazine People. There had been talks with Hollywood producers who wanted to win us for small roles in their films. It had seemed that in the USA, as well as elsewhere, all doors were open to us. Yet, suddenly, nobody was interested in me anymore. The media wrote me off. Totally.

And there was more: Shortly before the fight, I had parted company with my long-standing coach Fritz Sdunek. Also, Vitali and I had left our boxing promoter Universum—albeit voluntarily—after many years.

I was alone.

Practically all my companions turned away from me. The negatives mounted up. Yet it was the fact that my brother no longer believed in my ability that weighed on me the most. After all it was him to whom I had always wanted to prove that I was the better boxer. Now he was a world champion and I was a loser. For the first time in my life I was hugely demotivated and full of despair.

In retrospect this might sound strange: I had been successful for years and then two defeats are enough to bring down a tried and tested system for success? Yes, that's what it's like in boxing. Success in this sport is extremely short-lived. A single fight decides the world champion titles of the four big boxing associations. Unlike tennis there is no unified ranking system in which you move up or down and even after a defeat keep roughly the same position. Top or flop is the maxim in boxing, in each and every fight anew. If you lose the world champion's title, then the TV channels can very quickly lose interest in you. And with the TV coverage you lose the sponsors. Fighting your way back up afterwards can be extremely difficult.

Nonetheless, there was one positive that came from my defeats: the recognition that my career was finite. Beforehand, I would not have been able to accept that. Not at the age of 28! "Defeats will not dictate to me when my career ends," I said to myself, picked myself up and carried on. "I am going to show them!"

From that moment on, I turned my life as a professional boxer on its head and did everything differently: Until then it had been the promoters and other officials of the company who determined 98 percent of our day to day sporting life. It was them who chose the coach; them who took care of our nutrition, training opportunities and accommodation; them who selected opponents, locations and dates of the bouts; them who negotiated our advertising contracts. We were never consulted on any of these things. To a certain extent this was very agreeable because it freed us up to concentrate fully on the sport. On the other hand, the way it was done reduced us to fighting machines without a voice or a will of their own.

This is what I wanted to change now, even despite the will of my valued and beloved brother. After all, he had written me off and suggested that I retire.

In retrospect I realize that many around me thought me an arrogant brat who was bitter and resistant to advice. They felt I was too self-assured because I was not prepared to listen to them anymore. Yet I was doing what I considered right: to listen to my gut feeling and rely on the knowledge and experience that I had accumulated over the years; my expertise. I was so convinced of this that I even accepted clashing with my brother over it.

Apart from having a strong will, I was helped by another ability I have always had. My power of persuasion won over people whom I needed. I managed to get Emanuel Steward—who back then was considered a boxing guru—on my side as my permanent coach.

Similarly I won over Bernd Bönte, a former TV journalist and highly experienced and successful marketing professional with experience of the sport of boxing, whom I had worked with before. He believed in me and trusted me 100 percent. Since then he has not left my side and we are still working together. I employed a chef of my own, which nobody back then had done. I also signed up a physiotherapist, even though he had far less experience with boxers than his colleagues had, because I had spotted enormous potential in him. As another boxing first, I also hired my own cutman for my bouts. I made sure I got the best of the best.

The way in which I was working with people changed, too. While in Emanuel Steward I was employing one of the most experienced coaches in the sport, I did not want to delegate the preparation of the fights to him and take an absolute back seat, as boxers usually do. I worked out my strategy with him, made up the training schedule and decided the duration and frequency of my training. He looked after the actual boxing within the ring. In the beginning this was unfamiliar for him, but he was professional enough to go with it. "Wladimir's training is not about boxing, it's about tactics", he once said in an interview. "With him boxing turns into chess".

This was true: Even now I still spend a lot of time studying and analyzing my opponents because it matters to me psychologically and because I minutely fine-tune my training accordingly.

The biggest change, however, was happening behind the scenes. After we cancelled our contract with the promoter, the organization and management of our fights were in the hands of my brother and myself. Already in 2003 we had had the foresight to set up K2 Promotions, but up until now it had not been more than an empty shell of an organization. "Do we really want to do this?" Vitali had asked me doubtfully at the start. "Isn't this too much effort?" However, we concluded together: "We can do this!" We decided not to extend the contract with our longstanding promoter as we were convinced that we could do a better job ourselves. Vitali was the reigning world champion and I the hungry challenger. We began staffing K2 as a promotion company. Together with Bernd Bönte we looked for a supportive partner and found Sportfive, a Hamburg sporting rights marketer. In this way we retained the final decision about what opponents to choose, how many bouts to enter and what advertising partners to select.

However, all of this carried a considerable financial risk for me. Vitali announced his temporary retirement at the end of 2004 as a variety of injuries forced him to take almost four years out from the sport. Consequently, many decisions and the whole responsibility rested on me from then on. Yet this did not daunt me in any way. My goal was to regain my world champion's title and to prove everyone wrong who had written me off, especially my brother. He had always been my role model. After our big argument at the training camp we had distanced ourselves from each other. Although I had not yet demonstrated that I was the better boxer, I had at least shown him that I could reach all of my goals when I was the driving force; when I did not rush heedlessly into things but instead motivated myself with the best possible preparation and all of the expertise available within me.

Luckily my faith in myself was rewarded. I won the next bout and from then on things were steadily looking up until eventually I was the number one in several boxing associations.

After that I was sure: I can rely on my experiences. They have become the guideline that shows me the way. They tell me which decisions I may need to revisit and question in order to be able to follow my path with conviction, so that I can strongly and sustainably stand by my decisions

I understood that I am not only good at boxing, but that I am also capable of transferring my knowledge to other areas and applying it to think and act as a businessman. I have significantly more expertise than I had previously been aware of. I carry a whole wealth of knowledge and experiences within me that I just need to call upon. The next few years would demonstrate that I could transfer this expertise not just to business but also into totally different areas.

R—Rightness
Rightness, Developed According to My Ethical Guidelines

"Be a role model through ethical behavior"

Especially in Germany, at the start of my boxing career, boxing had an image problem and was not often thought of as a sport characterized by fairness or respect. Interestingly, in England and the USA both the image of and the interest in boxing were totally different to that in Germany. Vitali and I thought this was a sad and utterly incomprehensible state of affairs. Boxing is, after all, one of the oldest Olympic sports. We set out to restore its good reputation.

Among the values we had been taught at home were not just fairness and respect, but also acting ethically, justice, and broad-mindedness. To us it was a matter of necessity to carry these values over into our sport and not to conform. We were out to improve the reputation of boxing through the way we appeared and behaved.

So if, for example, my next opponent bad-mouthed me and tried to make me lose my self-control with his insults, I made sure I kept my composure. I have never approved of starting rumors just to demoralize another sportsperson. In my mind, the fight only takes place in the ring, not at press conferences or in the tabloid press.

I am convinced to the core that we should go through life upright, honestly, and openly, and that we should treat each other that way, too. This was already visible at the beginning of my career when I was 19 and boxed for Flensburg in the German national league. My club had arranged two exhibition bouts against the Ukrainian national side, which included Vitali. My countrymen had arrived by bus from Kiev and we were all sitting together on the train going west towards the North Sea, where the event was going to be held. The coach told us about the planned sequence and paired up me for BC Flensburg with Vitali as my Ukrainian opponent in the heavyweight category.

To both of us this was totally out of the question. We had given our promise to our mother never to fight each other.

This we stuck to; we would never have considered doing otherwise. Both my coach and the sponsor tried to change our minds, but without success. "But it is just an exhibition bout", they said. Yet, even in an exhibition fight we have to raise our fists against each other, was our answer. "You could just pretend", they tried next. Yet we did not want to do that, either. "That would mean cheating the audience", we said. Luckily they accepted our decision and allowed us to fight the respective side's light-heavyweight boxer.

Dishonesty, dubious behavior or criminality were out of the question for me. Yet, it was true that there had been temptations when I was young, after the break-up of the Soviet Union in the early 1990s. Times were tough. Many of the things that had already been scarce, like food, clothing, cars, alcohol, or tobacco, became scarcer still. People earning their money through honest work were not automatically paid any more than they had been under the Soviet system. Some did not have enough for themselves and their families even just survive.

As always when a country is going through upheaval and the political and economic order still needs to establish itself, criminal structures developed. This led to a situation where some of my former schoolmates became quite rich very quickly, by dubious means. At the same time I noticed that strong, self-confident men—athletes similar to my brother and myself—were moving in criminal circles. We received offers of questionable morality and, although these provided a brief moment of thrill, they never really posed a temptation for us. At no time did I consider leaving the straight and narrow and jettisoning the values my family had imbued in me.

First and foremost it was sport that made me stand firm. The sports boarding school and later on the sports science degree kept me very busy in terms of my time and thus occupied and distracted me. I had clear sporting aims and as a highlight enjoyed regular trips abroad, so I was happy with my life. I remember preparing for the Olympic Games in 1996: I was in Kiev after the German league season was over, training for the event in Atlanta. It was tough because I had suffered from food poisoning and had also had high blood pressure for several months. Nonetheless, I gave it my everything and worked like mad to get fit. My then coach dropped me off at one of the main roads out of Kiev as part of my stamina training. I ran 20 km back into town along this road. Considering my battered health, this was quite torturous. Along the way I was overtaken by several of my former schoolmates driving along in expensive cars, shouting arrogant boasts at me and gesturing through their open windows. Obviously they had made a lot of money in shadowy ways and had the connections to buy luxury cars like these, which would have been unaffordable to us.

I found this state of affairs hard to bear. I had spent years working hard both on my sporting career and academically. All just so that these boys, who were the same age as me, were passing me in expensive cars and overtaking me materially?

One day, I swore to myself, I was going to make it. I would be able to afford a modern car like that without having to do crooked business. I was going to manage to make it the right way, I was sure.

I have to admit that it took a while for the frustration to subside and for me to realize how others had come into this sort of money, and that is how I learnt to distinguish clearly between good and bad behaviors. My parents had always led by example and demonstrated through their own lives what it meant to tell the truth and to behave in a morally correct manner. Our environment however—irrespective of where my father was stationed, be it Kiev, Kazakhstan, Kyrgyzstan or Czechoslovakia—was ideologically tinged and thus only to a limited amount bound by ethical behavior.

In elementary school we were encouraged to snitch on other children if they did not behave in the spirit of communism. Also, we were expected to apologize to "Uncle Lenin" for everything, however small, even if it was just that we had forgotten our homework.

By the time I was a teenager I realized that those in power were to all intents and purposes brainwashing us. When Vitali, for example, returned from his first trip to the USA with our national team, he told us excitedly about the cities there, the sports halls, shopping malls, and all the things you could buy there. However, the usual reaction back home was: "Vitali, you don't actually believe that they live like that, do you? That's all just for show and they built it all and staged it for you to see. It's all just pretense, like Potemkin villages." As I got older it became ever clearer to me that the population back home was being fed deliberate misinformation and untruths. I understood that this propaganda was an integral part of the self-concept of communism and decided not to share this attitude. As a sportsperson, anyhow, I could see another aspect to all this. True to the Olympic spirit I wanted to get to know and appreciate other people and peoples and their countries—utterly irrespective of whatever political system they lived under.

I remember one occasion that wonderfully illustrates how our parents exemplified their values in their everyday lives. At the time I did not, of course, really attribute quite such significance to it. At the time we were living in Czechoslovakia where my father was stationed. I must have been about eight at the time. One afternoon we were in the car with him and met a Czech man on a moped who had run out of petrol.

Soviets were not particularly popular there at the time and we were easily identified as such because of my father's military vehicle. Yet he flagged us down and asked us for help. Without any hesitation my father siphoned off some gas from his tank and gave it to the moped rider. My father then politely turned down the proffered payment, for one simple reason: He did not want to enrich himself from something that was not his to start with. This was his duty vehicle after all. He just wanted to help the Czech man and did not expect anything in return.

I still remember how happy I was that my father gifted the Czech man the gas because we as Soviets did not have a good reputation there. I was proud because he had countered our poor image with something positive and had done the right thing.

G—Globalism
Globalism as a Globally Oriented, Holistic Way of Thinking and Acting

"Traveling is the best college life has to offer"

I see myself as a citizen of the world. In my private life I want to be able to travel wherever I want. As an athlete I want to be able to fight wherever I think it sensible. As a businessman I want to be able to do business wherever the opportunity arises, and as a mentor share my knowledge wherever I find the best environment for it. This attitude and my openness take me to a wide range of countries, from Germany and Switzerland to the UK, from Ukraine to the USA.

Yet it was a long way to get to this point. As a child of the Soviet Union I was living in a world of tight limits. Traveling was not something the people around me did, let alone were allowed to. Not to neighboring countries and very definitely not to the West. Only very few were allowed to do that.

This state of affairs made me curious even when I was still a child. I wanted to know what the world beyond the borders of our city and our country looked like. Very early on I yearned to travel. I wanted to look beyond my own backyard and find out how people lived on the other side of the globe. I itched to leave my limited world to gain both a better overview and a broader perspective. Maybe that is the reason I loved reading and re-reading Daniel Defoe's Robinson Crusoe over and over again.

Certainly, my family counted among the privileged ones in those times. Due to my father's job with the Soviet forces we moved house regularly. Come to think of it, we were constantly on the move: I was born in Kazakhstan, and moved to Czechoslovakia when I was six because my father was stationed there. Within four years I moved school twice. In 1986, when I was ten, we moved to Kiev. Four years after that I started at the sports boarding school.

From then on I really did start traveling the world. My schoolmates and I were crisscrossing the Soviet Union for events and later on also the Eastern Bloc countries and even the West.

When I was 15, I went to Germany for the first time, for international contests in the cities of Trier and Konz. I was without my family, just with my fellow athletes and attendants. Everything registered so clearly with me. It was the small things that fascinated me: colors, shapes, smells ... —everything was different.

If I revisit those days in my mind, I can immediately see why it was this that made such an impression on me. In the Soviet Union everything was uniform and monochrome, mostly in greys and black. Everyone wore similar clothes, similar shoes. If you had a car, it was the same model as the neighbors'. We lived in identical apartments. We children went to the same schools, sat on the same chairs and used the same exercise books. Everything looked the same. It was an ocean of similarity without any hint of individual taste. Even the bread we ate looked the same everywhere, and there were only three types, white, brown, and black, whether in Novosibirsk in Siberia or in Kiev. I found this frustrating.

In the West I did not know where to look first. I was especially drawn to colors. Whenever orange juice was served with a meal, I had it. I could not get enough of it both because I liked the taste and because it had an international feel to it. At home there was no such drink.

I also remember the bright yellow Walkman that Sony had brought out. It was such a cool, easy to carry tape player with headphones. Lots of athletes in the West were using it when jogging or during breaks in training. I was thrilled.

Even more impressive to me were Western cars. They looked so modern! They were available in so many different shapes and colors, nothing like our own models. Moreover, nearly every grown-up seemed to own one.

For me, traveling to Germany was like traveling into the future. Consequently, the return home felt like being transported to the past. While the Soviet Union was a leading power in many areas of research, was able to fly to the moon and to build nuclear weapons, nonetheless the everyday life of its people was rather backward.

I wanted to escape this boring monotony as often as possible and see more of the world. It was not just the products and designs that I liked. I wanted to get to know the people and interact with them. How did they live, what moved them, what did they enjoy, and in how far did their concerns and worries differ from ours? At first, this was difficult because of the language barrier, but if you really want to make contact then you will find a way to communicate.

When I moved to Germany permanently at the age of 20, I got to grips with the language quite quickly. Of course I still have an accent even now and I do occasionally find particular words difficult to pronounce. Yet it was of the utmost importance to me to be able to communicate and to exchange ideas with others.

What I had imagined came true: Boxing really did enable me to get to know other areas, countries and cultures. I learnt lots that my peers at home were not able to see or experience until years later. My experiences during my travels helped me not just to form a different opinion about everyday life in and the reality of the USSR; they also opened up a lot of new possibilities for me and enriched my mind enormously.

The traveling itself, however, was sometimes quite hard work. There was no luxury or comfort involved in the early years. We used an old bus wherever we went. We stayed in no-frills accommodation. Sometimes we were on the road for days in order to get in the ring somewhere. I didn't mind this at all. To be honest, I did not even notice it. I loved getting out of my usual surroundings. Traveling really is the best college life has to offer, I would say in retrospect.

When I journeyed to the USA for the Olympic Games in Atlanta, my biggest wish came true. Not just was this a once-in-a-lifetime kind of event, but it was also the very first time I went to North America. When I started my career as a professional athlete, I traveled more frequently and further: I visited Hong Kong, flew to the Rocky Mountains to go snowboarding and went on our first family vacation outside the Soviet Union with my parents and Vitali: to Gran Canaria. Vitali and I taught ourselves how to kitesurf there.

All of this was only possible because we had decided to take up boxing when we were boys; because we were successful at what we believed in.

There is something else I connect with "globalism": a holistic approach to thinking and acting, a 360-degree view. I have also been eager to learn. When I did not understand something, I searched out someone who could explain it to me until I had understood every last detail. I am still like that. I love discussing matters with people who know more about certain topics than I do. I love understanding their way of thinking and getting to learn from them. If a topic grabs me, then I educate myself with books or online. That is the way in which I try to deepen my understanding and to learn more. I also want to find out about the different levels and perspectives involved in the subject at hand by building on my existing knowledge and, where possible, to establish connections. I find this fulfilling.

Traveling was a good teacher in this respect, as were the endless games of chess with my brother: imagine yourself in your opponent's place. What does he see that you maybe can't at that moment? Maybe you are too wrapped up in yourself and therefore miss the obvious. The art is to put yourself in your opponent's position; to intuit his next move and to act accordingly.

This behavior I also transfer to other areas. In everything I do, I always consider the consequences first. What is the second step that is set into motion by the first? Before I go into negotiations I put myself into the other party's position. What is their aim? What pressure may they be facing, where is their pain threshold and where are the so-called win-win possibilities? If I were to focus only on myself then in all likelihood I would not find an optimal solution.

There is a wealth of examples to demonstrate a 360-degree view. A prerequisite in all of them is that we do not act in the heat of the moment and not just focus on one single aspect, but that we think and act multidimensionally and always make ourselves aware of the consequences beforehand.

O—Optimism
Optimism: Always Thinking Positively and with Vision

"I know no problems"

I am a dyed-in-the-wool optimist. No matter what the issue is, I always see the positives before I even notice the negatives. I value light-heartedness and try to banish bad moods or melancholy. I most like surrounding myself with cheerful, happy people with a positive attitude towards problem solving and I very much avoid grumblers and pessimists who find fault with everything.

Of course this does not mean that bad news does not put me in a reflective mood. When this happens, I like to be all by myself for a while to sort my thoughts. In my mind I then do what is known as a SWOT analysis: I reflect on my *strengths* and *weaknesses* and make myself aware of the *opportunities* and *threats*. From all these I then deduce what route to take next. I never cave in to looming obstacles or let them stop me. On the contrary, as an athlete I see them as challenges and get excited at the prospect of mastering them. I am even filled with an ever increasing feeling of anticipation at being able to prove to myself and the rest of the world I am not going to let anything mess up my plans easily.

When I was at the height of my career and lost not one, but two bouts in a row that really was a bitter experience, but I learned from it and single-mindedly set about trying to win back my world championship titles. In my life as a businessman, if I make a wrong decision I analyze the situation together with my team. I do my homework, as I call it, and try to emerge from the situation in a stronger position; in a positive mood; optimistic and confident; ideally even with a vision.

My optimism does not spring from the defeat but from the experience that I will achieve much less with a negative frame of mind. It is a fundamental decision one has to make whether to approach things positively and thereby to infect others with one's positivity. A long time ago I decided—at first unconsciously, but then very consciously—that I did not want to be counted among the grumblers. Time is too precious to waste it by grumbling.

I think I probably got this way of looking at life from my father's side of the family. Until he died in the summer of 2011 my father was an unshakeable optimist. Despite the cancer he had been suffering from for a long time, he was full of life and positivity. His mother had survived the holocaust and grown up in hard times, yet had a mischievous twinkle in her eye all her life.

When I was still very young, I frequently encountered the military humor that surrounded the sphere my father worked in. As both my parents worked and there was no kindergarten I could go to, my father sometimes took me to work with him. The soldiers looked after me there; they were my babysitters.

I had not started speaking by the time I was three—I spent a lot of time alone at home, which was not unusual at the time, but probably not at all helpful in terms of my speech development—and the soldiers wound me up with it. One afternoon they were trying to motivate me to talk by telling me swear-words and asking me to repeat them. They had a kind of competition going as to who could entice me to say my first word.

As a matter of fact, this worked after a while: One term, an unkind word used for women, caught my ear and I managed to repeat it. The men were beside themselves with joy. I was very proud because I thought I had done something really good; so proud, in fact that I kept repeating the word and would not stop. This made them laugh even more.

My father, however, was less enthused when he came to pick me up and made his unhappiness clear to the soldiers in no uncertain terms. I did not care. All I was concerned with was repeating that swear word over and over. Soon, Vitali was refusing to leave the house with me or look after me. He was at the end of his tether and felt embarrassed by me. My parents, too, were fast losing patience.

It was my grandma who solved it in the end. She told me that using swear words was bad and that these words needed to be punished and destroyed to make them "disappear." Together we thought up and tried lots of ways to get rid of the forbidden word. To begin with I spat the word into a pot that we put on the cooker in order to make the term boil away.

As that did not help, we put in into a frying pan and fried it at a high heat. After that we put it in the oven to burn it totally. To top it all off, we gave it to our dog to chew it up so that it might finally disappear from my vocabulary. Much to the relief of everyone involved, this long-winded procedure was crowned by success.

It took a while for me to stop swearing. What I remember about it, however, is how much fun I had with my grandma. While everyone else was annoyed, she approached the problem in a relaxed and humorous way. For a three-year-old such as me that way was likely to be the most successful in any case, I would think.

After this episode, the soldiers did not teach me any more swear words. They did, however, like to tell me jokes. These were typical army jokes: harmless and silly, rarely with a strong punch line, but perfect for brightening dull everyday life. As a child I loved these jokes.

Without even noticing, the soldiers showed me that we do not need much to make life better or easier; and that this is always a matter of attitude: Do I want to be bored or have fun? Do I want to see the bad or the good in a given situation? Do I want to stand still? Or do I want to move and get ahead?

Over the years I got to try out how much easier it is for me to reach my goal if I go about it in a good mood, with charm, self-confidence and joy. For example I always approached negotiations convinced that they were going to end well, however inauspicious the early indications.

To give you an example: During my first season in the German national league I was to earn 1,000 DM for each bout, 500 DM more for each win by points and an additional 500 DM for a knockout win.

From my point of view that was a lot of money, loads of money actually. Yet I wanted to try to negotiate a better arrangement still. "What would I get if I were to win all 15 bouts this season through knockouts?" I asked my then sponsor, the chairman of BC Flensburg and entrepreneur Harald Uhr. "You would never manage that" was his reply. "Let's do it then," I suggested with a grin. "If I win by knocking out every one of my opponents, I get an additional bonus of 10,000 DM." Harald Uhr looked at me incredulously but agreed nonetheless. He did not believe that I would manage that, I could see it plainly on his face—but I was equally sure that I would manage it.

Our relationship was built on trust and this enabled me to go back to Harald Uhr a week later with another request. He had found me a flat in the northeastern part of town, 5km away from the training venue. He probably thought that I was going to walk that distance every day. I, however, wanted a car. I put on a friendly and charming face and told him straight: "Harald, I need a car". Yet again, he did not turn me down and a few days later an orangey-red Opel Rekord was parked outside my flat. I was happy and did not mind at all that it was his mother's old car.

I never thought about whether the club treated me more generously than its other sportspeople or whether I had special status somehow. Yet it must have been like that. I recently, after many years, met my old sponsor Harald Uhr—who had invited me to Flensburg and enabled me to start my career there—and he gave me the explanation: He had understood that I would go a long way in boxing and therefore felt that I was a wise investment for his money. Also, he liked the fact that I did not come begging, but negotiated self-confidently and challengingly but in a friendly way. What I did not know was that Vitali had already spoken to Harald back then and cautioned him not to try to rip me off. The fact that I ended up gaining far more than previously arranged, amused Harald in a way. In the end he even threw in monthly plane ticket to Kiev for me to go and visit my family regularly.

Ever since then this has been my modus operandi: Using charm and sound arguments I try, even after the negotiations have finished, to arrange a little extra bargain that challenges me to go the extra mile and to try my hardest. In doing so, I make sure I do not come across as brazen, but demand just enough for it still to be acceptable for the other party. If they agree, then I am a very satisfied negotiator—just like the party, too.

"Business is not only about making money," is a well-known mantra in the business world, and I fully agree with it. It matters how I demand something, how I present myself and how I phrase what I say. If your appearance and tone are positive, respectful and appreciative, then it is much easier to reach an agreement.

Quite possibly I also need luck on my side. By this I don't mean luck in the sense of pure happy chance, which I consider just too random for me to believe in. Luck is something that I can influence positively to a certain extent. My arrangement with my Flensburg sponsor went as follows: I really did win all 15 bouts by knock-out. However, we had not fixed the bonus in writing and therefore he could have easily pulled out of the arrangement. "So," I asked Harald Uhr at the end of season party, "do you still remember our little agreement?" "Yes, I do," he answered, "even though I never in my life expected you to actually manage that. But yes, you'll get your bonus." And he pulled out an envelope and gave me the money in cash.

I was on cloud nine.

S—Sustainability
Sustainability: Taking the Long-term View and Being Environmentally Conscious

"I am not interested in quick success"

I am not a fan of nine-day wonders, they get forgotten too quickly. To me it only makes sense to invest my time and energy in long-term projects. Because experiences and successes add up, build on each other and cross-fertilize. Any other way I would not have managed to become a multiple world champion in boxing. With a bit of luck you might manage to gain that title once; there are lots of examples of that. To remain at the top longer term, however, requires you to demonstrate foresight and sustainability.

Long-term success in boxing is incredibly hard to manage. If I win a bout and gain a world champion's title from one of the four major boxing associations then the success and satisfaction don't last long. For a little while I might think that I am on top of everything, but that feeling of "conquest" is only temporary. I have to turn my attention to the future again.

That situation is comparable to many other areas, such as the music industry. For a musician it is not sufficient nowadays to issue a hit record. Ahead of the launch, the artist and their team should also align their marketing and communications in such a way that the fans will not just buy or download the songs but will also be primed to buy concert tickets and merchandising. Without positioning themselves accordingly and planning sustainably for the long term, the artist will often not be able to withstand the enormous pressures from within and without. The consequence is that they cannot spend all their time and effort on their real job, which is composing and recording music.

There is a difference between musicians and me as a boxer: Musicians have weeks or even months to produce new songs. In boxing, on the other hand, success is a matter of minutes. At most I have twelve times three minutes to defeat my opponent. 36 minutes that decide success or failure. That requires not just optimal preparation from me, but also a killer instinct; it requires the absolute desire and determination to leave the ring as the winner.

Yet how do I keep this instinct raw even though I have been successful for a long time? It is only natural for us to become complacent and a little ponderous if we have grown used to success. The killer instinct becomes sedated. Many companies are all too aware of this challenge to keep the organization and the employees yearning for more even when the business is virtually running itself due to its position as market leader. Steve Jobs, the founder of Apple, aptly advised: "Cannibalize yourself before someone else does". Companies need a culture that corresponds to this challenge; a culture that sustainably demands competition and top results, that supports innovative and business-minded workers and that condemns stagnation.

As an athlete, my attitude is similar. However, business failure only becomes visible after weeks or months, while a boxer's defeat is immediately obvious. When I am in the ring, I am alone with no-one to hide behind.

In my experience the answer to these challenges, namely to be hungry to win in the short term and motivate yourself anew over and over again in the long term, lies in focusing your mind. In the best case this mental focus can develop into a real strength, which is why I have been working on it since the beginning of my career and use a number of techniques for mental training.

It was my PhD supervisor and mentor, sports science professor Viktor Volkov, who taught me the basic and enduring lesson that the body and the mind are both part of the same and that I can only achieve sustainable success if both body and mind are healthy. He started teaching me when I was just 16 years old. That was the age I started my university studies in Ukraine. He was the first person who had a real impact on how I functioned. He taught me that athletes need to feed not just their body but also their brain. I learnt from him that balanced nutrition is an absolute must and that there are phases during which the body and the mind are resilient to the maximum, but others when they are not.

At the same time, he also ensured that my academic studies were a sustainable success. He was my adviser for my PhD thesis, which dealt with pedagogical control of young athletes. I was fascinated by the topic and enjoyed researching it. When I had to defend my thesis in front of 13 professors, however, I was unsure if I was going to be able to convince them. "Use your experience, your practice", my adviser suggested. "They may well know a lot about the theory, but they do not know nearly as much about your work as you do. You know the practical side because you conducted the study." This advice I have carried with me all my life.

Even today when I give a lecture to leaders and entrepreneurs, I still stick to that maxim: No-one is better placed than myself to talk about my experiences in sports. Furthermore, nowadays I can credibly talk about what it means to apply my expertise from my sport to the world of business. Back when I defended my thesis, this method worked well, too, and I was awarded a doctorate. Many people from the world of boxing were amazed and confused that Vitali and I, despite all our sporting successes, still kept up our academic careers, too. I, however, never questioned it because we had been raised to use sustainable thinking to guide our actions at all times. I also know that the doctorate and the title that came with it have often come in handy since.

I am still in contact with my PhD advisor. To me, this is also an aspect of sustainability: to stay at the side of people who supported me and accompanied me on my path. Professor Volkov lives in the same town in Ukraine as my godfather. When I go to visit one, I also meet up with the other. My advisor takes a lot of interest in my development. He was very pleased that in 2016 I initiated a certificate course at the University of St. Gallen in Switzerland. He enthusiastically swaps ideas with me about the content and methods of the course and offers suggestions and support.

The important things in life should last a long time and need to be quality, as I learnt from my father. Half a century ago he built a house for my grandma in Kazakhstan. Due to a lack of clay, he used dirt mixed with grass and plastered the walls with that. He dug a well, built a shower and toilets, and even built an impressive gate at the entrance to the plot. He managed all of this on his own, without large machinery or anything like that. I went there with Vitali a few years ago for the first time in ages. I was impressed because the house was still standing and showing no structural problems at all. Of course, it was not in a good state on the inside because it had not been lived in for a very long time. On the outside, however, everything still looked fine. At the entrance we could even still see an emblem we had chosen for our family all those years ago: a rising sun that shone over the door.

My father paid such close attention to quality and durability that my mother got cross with him at times: When we were living in a flat in Prague, he was to hang a carpet on the wall as a decoration. Instead of just nailing it to the wall, he took the task very seriously, chose some thick planks of wood, fixed the carpet to them and drilled large holes in the wall. My mother just rolled her eyes: "It's only supposed to last a couple of years", she said. "We'll never be able to get that off again". She was right about that. I had a look at the flat a while ago. Everything had been taken down apart from the carpet that was still hanging on that wall. I tried to loosen it but it would not budge. And it was not like I was out of strength...

Sustainability guides me in all matters, large or small. Just like my grandma's house was durable, I wished for my success to be sustainable, not just in boxing but beyond. That is the reason why I and my team already started to plan years ago what my career should be after the end of my sporting career. We developed a university course, in which I pass on my insights gained from being a professional sportsperson to managers and entrepreneurs. Methods, products and services are in the pipeline. Their credibility rests on my decades-long successful career as a boxer, and they are being developed on the basis of my experience so that one development can cross-fertilize and benefit from another. This is totally in the spirit of sustainability.

Uncomplexity: Easy to Explain and Easy to Understand

"Everything ingenious is simple"

"Keep it simple" is the maxim that Steve Jobs installed as the guiding principle at Apple. With this he captured the spirit of the time and created a massive market because he was the first in that industry to create simply styled products that were perfectly thought through and intuitive to use. Albert Einstein, after all, was convinced that "if you cannot explain it in simple terms, then you do not understand it well enough."

Both of these statements I subscribe to fully. I greatly appreciate clear statements and efficient solutions. I neither like speeches that fail to get to the point nor products that require complicated explanations. Everything ingenious is also simple. Neither do I understand people's vanity. Rather than wasting time, I prefer to concentrate on useful and important things instead of circumstantial matters.

My professional life, for instance, I structure clearly according to simple aims: What do I want to achieve in the short, medium, and long term? These aims are very concrete and ideally include a place and date. In my past, the next goal was always winning the upcoming fight. Now, other topics have joined the aims, for example to further substantiate the method of the course I run at the University of St. Gallen so that the questions left open last year do not come up again.

Once I have reached one goal, I can start addressing the next. One after the other, in a very focused and structured way. This is so that my whole team and I myself can invest our energy in this one goal and reach it efficiently. If I see how employees' targets are defined in many companies, it's enough to make me feel rather dizzy: There is a veritable multitude of targets for the next twelve months, and some of them are so cryptic or so wide-ranging that hardly anyone knows what they mean. As a consequence, they are never achieved.

As a soldier's son I learnt about clear statements and instructions from a very early age. At our home nobody beat about the bush. If there was a problem, then it was brought up and addressed. If my brother or

I had an issue, then solutions were found for it. Nowadays I appreciate the advantages of that approach. Back then, however, I did on occasion moan about these house rules.

To give you an example, my father had given me and my brother Vitali the job of keeping his uniform shoes and belt clean and in good condition. After cleaning them we were to provide feedback that we had finished the job. One evening, Vitali and I were lying in bed—which we had to share—at around midnight when my father came home. I must have been five or six years old but he treated me as if I was older. He woke us up, turned the lights on and held his shoes right in front of our noses. Then he scolded us: "Why have my shoes not been cleaned? Get up!" This episode repeated itself once or twice more that night either because the shoes were not sufficiently shiny or because we did not report back that the task had been completed.

As uncomfortable as I found such situations at the time, I have to admit that they left an impression on me. In addition to my preference for clear statements, I also always pay attention to having clean shoes and well-kept clothes. I even like to iron my own shirts because in my mind no-one does that as well as I do it myself.

I also ask all of my staff to "report" to me. They can just give me their thumbs up that they have received a task and understood it. As I can then be sure that this task will be dealt with, I am able to cross it off my mental list automatically.

The conviction that an orderly environment helps to have an orderly mind was always present in my childhood home. "The rest of your day will look the same way your bed looks when you leave in the morning," my mother used to admonish me constantly. There was therefore not a single day that I did not shake out my blankets and straighten them, even if I got out of bed late. I still do that today, and that is because I think it is absolutely true: If I leave my apartment in a state of chaos, then there is a high likelihood that the day ahead will be just as chaotic. For the same reason I always keep my desk tidy.

I am so used to my family's clarity and the way we approach things that I am sometimes caught by surprise at how poor other people can be at getting to the point or at how they state something emotionally without having thought their message through clearly and without phrasing it intelligibly.

I was impressed very positively with Bill Clinton whom I encountered twice within a short time at events a few years ago. This former President of the United States had traveled to Ukraine and to the German city of Munich to speak in front of large audiences. This was the first time that I had seen him in this kind of set-up, and I was impressed. He neither spoke the language of his audience not was he close to them in any way, and yet Clinton managed beautifully to arouse affinity and enthusiasm from his listeners.

In Munich I had the chance to speak to him after his talk and asked him how he had managed to build such rapport with the audience. He shared three golden rules with me:

- Do your homework: Practice every speech, no matter how short or long it is.
- Put yourself in your audience's shoes and ask yourself: Where are they coming from, what are they interested in?
- And most importantly: Try to bring across any topic, however complex it may be, in a simple way. Do not be so stupid as to try to make things look more complicated, hoping to appear really clever. That way you would just waste your chance to move your audience and inspire them.

M—Maximum

Maximum: Always Striving to Achieve the Best and the Optimum

"More is possible"

It is like a hunger that can never be sated. I need challenges, over and over, always new challenges. I am not voracious, but my appetite is everlasting. Once I have achieved one goal, I search for the next. It is not sufficient to just about reach these goals; I want to conquer them in the best way possible, always, in any situation. "Failure is not an option," was my motto for a long time when I was preparing for upcoming fights. I'd rather have died than come second. After my defeat in late 2015 I simplified this for my next fight. "Obsessed" then became—and remains—my mantra to prepare myself for my next goal, the bout.

Both may sound drastic, but they fit my convictions. From a young age I started trying to get more from a situation than other people do. The Soviet Union, where I grew up, was a country defined by queuing. We had to queue to buy bread. We had to queue to wait for our pay packet. We queued to get into the swimming pool. We queued obediently and patiently. If someone tried to push in, there were angry looks and the wrongdoer was sent to the back of the queue. It did not matter whether you were in a hurry. Interestingly there weren't actually very many who were in a hurry.

I quickly worked out that as a child there was the odd opportunity to make your way further up the queue. My big eyes, happiness and innocent smiles nicely managed to soften up hearts. If I also had a good story as a reason, which sounded too ridiculous not to be true, then occasionally I even made it right to the front. Having worked my magic on the others in the line to let me go to the front, I then even managed to melt the heart of the strict lady at the tills most of the time.

The object of this was not that I wanted to cheat others or get a special deal for myself as a matter of principle. Rather, I saw a goal and wanted to achieve it. It did not matter to me how inventive I had to be to get there.

There were a number of qualities I could draw on to get the best or the most out of a situation for myself and my family. Charm was one of them, as well as relentlessness and tenacity.

I was eight years old when I tried to persuade my parents finally to buy me a bike of my own. Up until then, Vitali and I shared one. He sat on the saddle while I had to make do with the crossbar. I felt incredibly silly riding along virtually on my brother's lap. This needed to end! Unfortunately, as my mother told me, we had no money to buy a second bike.

We were living in Czechoslovakia at the time, and I spotted a classified ad for second-hand bikes of the Ural brand in the newspaper. I knew and admired the brand Ural, which came from the Soviet Union. As chance would have it, the seller lived right in our neighborhood.

I begged my mother to allow me to go and have a look at the bikes. She just repeated time and again: We have no money for a second bike. In the end she granted me an amount that she would be able to let me have. This budget was ridiculously small. It would not even have been enough for the handlebar. Nonetheless, I got her permission and was on my way to the bike seller. I went on my own. Under no circumstances did I want anyone to go with me. In all seriousness I began to negotiate with the dealer.

I cannot remember whether he took me seriously or was just having me on. He went along with my bargaining. When I finally told him my available budget, he started laughing. "You must be joking," he told me. Yet I did not give up. Brandishing all my charm I asked him to lower the price. I did not lie and pretend that I would pay the money later. I would not have been able to do that and I did not want to, either. Instead, I told him just how important it was to me to have my own bike, and how much I hated wearing my brother's hand-me-down clothes and having to ride on the bar of his bike without ever being able to choose the destination myself.

Maybe this reminded him of his own childhood, or maybe he just wanted me to leave him in peace. Either way, it worked. He sold me the bike for the money I had offered, at a ridiculously low price. I did not mind in the slightest that it was an adult bike. I rode it standing up until my legs finally grew long enough to touch the ground when I sat on the saddle.

Business acumen and my eternal desire to get the most out of any given situation have been my driving force since my school days. I was about twelve when Vitali and I started selling pictures of film stars. Arnold Schwarzenegger and Sylvester Stallone were our heroes at the time, just as they were for lots of boys. Sadly we could not see their films either at the cinema or on TV.

Vitali had a camera and taught himself how to develop the films. Somewhere we had laid our hands on a magazine with pictures of the actors. We photographed the pictures, developed them and sold the resulting prints on the school yard for 20 kopeks. Our friends were proud to own a photo of an action hero from the West, and we were happy to earn so much money on the side. When I told Arnold Schwarzenegger about this a few years ago, he jokingly asked me for his share of the money we had earned.

In a similar vein I traded in "Spirit Royal" a few years later. I bought the spirit in large quantities and sold it on in smaller units to acquaintances and other people from my area. Interestingly, there was nothing remotely complicated or illegal about this at all. The spirits were available to everyone as it was a household product with many uses. Some used it for cleaning or for lighting fires, others for disinfecting or for cleaning hair. Some even drank it. Anyone could have run this little business. However, there were very few people with any business sense back then in our area. The Soviet economic order simply did not envisage proactiveness. People were not hungry, and their basic needs had been looked after automatically for too long. As a consequence, it was easy for me to make money with this kind of petty trade when I was a teenager.

As these examples show, I have always been different to my schoolmates and friends. I never cared about belonging, and neither did I want to have to do anything just to be accepted into a group. I always did my own thing—if possible, with my brother. I always had something I wanted to achieve: starting an undertaking, setting up projects, climbing a summit. It is still like that today: I always want more. I always want to achieve the best—in a clean and honest way.

Conclusion

- I started thinking early on about what I was going to do after my boxing career. Therefore I and my team developed the "career after the career".
- "Ergo Sum" is the guiding principle and the philosophy that I and my staff base our decisions on.
- My experiences in sport helped me become a successful entrepreneur.

3. I Am not a Dummy, I Can Walk by Myself

From Image Transfer to Expertise Transfer

My professional debut in Hamburg was exciting: having won at the Olympic Games in Atlanta, in November 1996 I signed a contract, together with Vitali, with a prestigious boxing promoter. Up until then I had always only boxed against amateurs, but now my opponents were experienced professionals. I was reassured by the fact that I could not just hold my own at their level but even do well. I achieved knockout wins in all fights I entered during my first year. This was despite the fact that by the usual boxing standards I competed in an enormous number of bouts that year, sixteen in total. Vitali had the same workload, which means that one of us Klitschkos was in a bout at least every other week.

This was our routine for two or three years: training, fight, training, fight. Initially, I did not question the high number of fixtures. I also accepted the fact that I was not allowed input into what opponent I was going to fight nor was given any information about the contracts. I was quite simply driven by my desire to be one of the best. Therefore, I concentrated all my attention on my training. In addition I did all the required sponsoring appearances and marketing duties, which were a part of mine and my brother's contracts with the promoter.

My first TV advert, which I remember with amazing clarity, was for a liver medication called "Heppa Besch". At the time, I was very pleased about my first TV appearance, but in retrospect I cannot help but ask myself what on Earth those responsible for this choice were thinking. Did a liver treatment really fit me and my image? Was it the right choice for what I embodied? This was something my promoter had not considered. There was no strategy on the promoting company's part and no plan about what the best way to market us might be. Its only interest was its baseline, without any concern about the short-termism of this kind of thinking.

After a while, dissatisfaction began to grow in me, at first very quietly and cautiously but over time it became ever louder and stronger. I began to realize: It was not just Vitali and I who ought to be grateful to our promoter for enabling us to start a professional career. The deal was based on reciprocity, on give and take, because the promoter profited from us, too. The German term for a promotion agency is "Boxstall", which literally translates as a "boxing stable". I do not like this term at all, but in this case it was absolutely appropriate because I was made to feel like a workhorse. Yet I wanted to be anything but a disenfranchised fighting machine. I felt that our promoter ought to let us have a say. I wanted to know what contracts he negotiated for us. In those years our contracts were essentially a "black box" to me: We were never given any information about how much money the promoter made through any of our bouts nor about how much he was prepared to spend to ensure quality at the events.

It took me four years to work my way up and compete at a title bout for the first time: I wanted to get that first world champion's belt for myself. By then I had gained some idea of what marketing opportunities there might be available for us. I had watched dozens of boxing events, had occasionally witnessed discussions with sponsors and knew just how incredibly important the TV broadcasts were for increasing one's reach. The broader the reach, the more interested the sponsors and the bigger the prize money for the fights. Our degree of celebrity had been increasing, and we were already well-known beyond the confines of our sport.

This was brought into sharp focus for me when I bought a BMW for my girlfriend and happened to start chatting to the staff at the car showroom in Hamburg. I told them that we, the "boxers", could do with new cars, too, and that BMW might be able to benefit from our celebrity status. This piqued the car producer's interest, which is why I referred my contacts at BMW on to my promoter to discuss the details. Without a lot of negotiations, the car company provided us with seven cars. I got one of them, the others ended up with my promoter. In return, BMW was able to present itself as a sponsor of ours. In theory this was a deal that all sides should have been happy with.

Yet our satisfaction only lasted until Vitali's next fight. The shorts that had been laid out ready for him carried a large Jaguar logo on the waistband. We could not believe our eyes. How was this possible? Everybody knew that BMW and Jaguar were competitors in the luxury market segment. Nobody had asked Vitali for his approval nor even just informed him. I was speechless. I felt incredibly ashamed and knew that I could not possibly reconcile the way this had been handled with my own ethics and values. This was not what Vitali and I were like. I was deeply embarrassed because BMW quite rightly got the impression that they could not rely on us as partners. The company had supported us, and yet we trampled all over the agreement—or at least, this is what it must have looked like from BMW's point of view.

At home we had been taught: If I give someone my word, then I have to keep it, even if I have to move heaven and earth. Our promoter, however, lacked any sensibility, and the manager in charge of boxing just shrugged his shoulders. No one at the promotion agency seemed to care that BMW were more than just a little displeased. Their only interest was to earn as much as they could on fight nights.

It was becoming ever clearer that we were following different strategic goals than the promotion agency. Vitali and I were interested in long-term success, but also in credibility, fairness and expertise. We wanted to be competent, valuable and reliable partners for businesses.

A few weeks later Vitali and I received a letter from Werner Baldessarini, who was chairman of Hugo Boss at the time. Baldessarini was an enthusiastic follower of boxing and wrote to us with the offer to kit us out and to dress us for 10,000 DM at the VIP shop at the Hugo Boss headquarters in Metzingen, Germany. I was excited and absolutely over the moon with his offer. Theirs was a fabulous brand and the offer such an honor.

Thus, I drove all the way to the south of Germany to pay a visit to this clothing company. Apart from the fact that I received wonderful suits, shirts and jackets, I was also treated to a meeting with Werner Baldessarini.

He enjoyed sharing with me his visions about how brands in general and boxing events in particular could be staged. I soaked up his words like a sponge and was inspired by his electrifying manner. For three quarters of an hour he enthused about Henry Maske, the light-heavyweight world champion for many years, and about the broadcasts of his fights on the German TV channel RTL. Initially I was amused by his enthusiasm, but he was right: The fights were more than purely a boxing bout; they were staged to look almost like an event. This was a novelty in Germany. Suddenly this was what I wanted, too.

Baldessarini was so enthusiastic about this topic that time just flew. We were passing the ball back and forth between us and started to imagine the perfect event down to the smallest details. He talked with such a lot of detail that I could clearly visualize his ideas. For the celebrity guests, he suggested, there should be a red carpet and a VIP area. The floor of the boxing ring should not be too dark because that was bad for televising the event. He thought white was a good color that would not flicker on TV screens. The ropes around the ring should be of a particular thickness and arranged in a particular way to enable adverts to be hung from then without impairing the audience's view of the boxers. The lights, colors, outfits, the walk-in song—everything had a role to play and should be planned consciously.

Of course, much of this I had heard before and had pondered in my head already. Nonetheless, Baldessarini expressed exactly what I felt: For quite a while I had been thinking about how our appearances could be improved, but unfortunately my ideas and visions fell on deaf ears with my promoter. Our bouts were broadcast on a public service TV channel, and I had to admit: the staging of our fights and the bouts by Henry Maske on a commercial channel were worlds apart. I thought it quite symptomatic that, of all people, a fashion designer with an interest in boxing was discussing with me how things could be improved, while no-one in my professional boxing environment was interested in this at all.

From this meeting with Werner Baldessarini grew a friendship that is still going strong today. Werner is a visionary, and ever since our first meeting he has been sharing his views and visions with us. Furthermore, we managed to secure Hugo Boss as our sponsor. This was a partnership to my liking. The company was a quality brand that was a great fit for our own brand values, our standards, and our image.

It was at this point that the feeling that I wanted more started to rise inside me. I had tasted blood and realized that there were people who shared my understanding of collaboration. They used it in order for both parties to benefit from each other's image. It was this kind of cooperation that I wanted to build in the future. My partners would, ideally, be able to use my image and our names, and at the same time I would offer them my expertise. I had learnt in the past that real and sustainable partnerships develop in just this way. I wanted to get away from transfer of the image and move into transfer of expertise.

My vision was that Vitali and I would become a brand ourselves.

Admittedly, back then this sounded like a daring plan. There were hardly any boxers who were brands. True, many had nicknames that referenced their boxing characteristics. However, for a boxer to embody specific values explicitly and to market these in a targeted way, sustainably and beyond the sport, was really rather unusual.

Yet the time was ripe for it. In Germany boxing had suffered from an unsavory image during the 1970s, 80s and into the 1990s. It was Henry Maske's success that changed this state of affairs. The media as well as his fans called him "gentleman" because his well-groomed looks and his classy appearance set him apart from most others in the sport.

The commercial TV channel RTL did its best to popularize the sport and make the bouts available to a larger audience. The image of the sport improved significantly.

We wanted to use this higher profile of boxing as well as our own popularity and attempt to position ourselves as a brand. In everything we did we tried to employ the highest standards of quality and to ensure that they were adhered to.

For us to go down this path, it was inevitable that we had to part ways with our promoter. We needed to be marketed individually to be able to implement this plan consistently and to have a say in decisions.

Unfortunately, this proved to be quite difficult. The promotion agency had no interest in letting us go early. The promoter came up with reason after reason why our contract kept being prolonged. If we were injured or ill, he drew on contractually agreed options to keep tying us to him. Working for him kept dragging on and on.

I remember a period about two and a half years after my first world champion's title. I had fought a lot of bouts within a short time and longed for a break from the sport. I was tired and suffered from a boxer's equivalent of burn-out. My promoter did not want to know, instead arranging the next fight, and just tried to placate me: "Don't you worry. We'll find a good opponent for you".

This "good opponent" turned out to be Corrie Sanders, a South African who was known to be an aggressive boxer with a formidable punch and a high capacity to tolerate being hit. I was angry that my promoter did not accept my wish for some time out. It was not even three months since I had defended my title in Las Vegas. I had to go ten rounds until I defeated my opponent by technical knockout. This time round I hoped for a faster victory.

I prepared the same way as always. However, when I saw my gloves in the changing rooms just before the bout, I lost my faith. For the first time ever there was advertising printed on them. I could not believe it. Texts or pictures on the gloves provide maximum distraction for a boxer. Why had no-one consulted me on this?

Annoyingly, there was no alternative as I could not change the gloves. This was the pair that the association had cleared for the bout. Therefore, I had no choice but to wear them. As always, Vitali was with me in the hours before the fight, and he helped me draw over the advertisements with a thick felt tip pen. I wanted to make sure my annoyance was clearly noticeable. This did not help much, though; I was still angry.

"I am fed up to my back teeth," I thought to myself. I wanted to defeat Sanders quickly and then take a vacation; to recover from the physical and psychological strain of the previous months and from the disappointment. However, this is not how it turned out: Sanders won, I lost. To make matters worse, my promoter had not included a rematch clause in the contract as would have been normal when voluntarily defending a title. The promoter would have had to pay a higher purse, which he did not want to do. Thus, I did not even have the chance of getting my world champion's title back. Misplaced greed on the part of the promoter had sunk the opportunity for a rematch. This was the last straw for me: I desperately wanted to follow my own path.

A few months previously, Vitali and I had founded our own promotion agency, K2 Promotions, with Tom Löffler as managing director. Up until my fight against Sanders it had only been a shell, but now we wanted to bring it to life.

When Vitali faced Corrie Sanders in Los Angeles in April 2004—he wanted to get the title for himself that I had lost to the South African not so long before—, this was the first fight that we marketed ourselves. The driving force behind this act of emancipation was definitely me. Vitali was rather daunted by the organizational effort we would have to face. To me, however, one thing was very clear: We would be able to market our bouts far more professionally than had been the case previously. We had the knowledge and the expertise needed to make it work.

We were sensible enough not to think we could do everything by ourselves. Bernd Bönte, who had a lot of experience and expertise in boxing as well as being a sports aficionado and former head of boxing at the pay-TV channel Premiere, found a supportive partner for us in Sportfive, a sports rights marketing company. Bönte took up a position as our manager at Sportfive and acted as our contact there. K2 Promotions got hooked up to Sportfive as a sort of "free agent" for events. The crucial difference for us was that, unlike previously, we now had the power to make decisions ourselves about the choice of opponents and the number and frequency of our bouts. We also selected our advertising partners ourselves and took up responsibility for our event management.

I have to admit it: the start was quite bumpy. After being defeated by Corrie Sanders and Lamon Brewster I did manage to fight my way back up, but it took some time. I came out the winner in my next fight, which took place against DaVarryl Williamson in fall 2004. However, this bout held so little attraction for our recently secured TV partner Premiere that they dropped us again immediately. When Vitali faced Danny Williams two months later, we still had no TV partner in Germany. "This is your fault," he reproached me. I had to admit that he was right, yet was still convinced we had done the right thing in leaving our promoter.

Vitali won his fight, which was broadcast on the public service channel ARD, but announced his retirement the following year. He had been plagued by injuries and had to endure multiple operations. In the end, he was to make a successful return to boxing in 2008, but we could not know this at the time of his retirement.

Our collaboration with Sportfive went very well. They had successfully grasped how to work with us as a brand. Whereas our previous promoter had simply sold our names willy-nilly to various sponsors, we were undertaking market research. We defined our brand values in order to be able to identify partners, products and services that were suited to us. Eventually, we also managed to enter into a TV partnership with ARD, and from 2006 onwards with the commercial RTL.

Over time, however, I started to notice that the criteria I attached to partnerships and projects were not fulfilled to a sufficient degree. I did not just want to be marketed, I wanted to positioned first. For this, long-termism, sustainability and quality mattered. I wanted to play an active role and provide input. I wanted to share my expertise and make it available to others.

In 2007 the time had come for me to end our collaboration with Sportfive. We had gained a wealth of experience by then, especially with regard to event marketing. I had thought through ever more precisely what I wanted and what I did not want. I had had lots of discussions with Vitali. "Is this really a step we should take?" he had asked me repeatedly. The workload we would have to shoulder was immense. "Is it going to be worth the effort?" we asked ourselves. I felt that we were perfectly prepared for becoming a totally independent outfit. We founded KLITSCHKO Management Group, KMG, as a company specializing in event marketing and sponsoring and ensured that our old associate and manager for many years, Bernd Bönte, joined us there. He is still the managing director and co-owner of the KLITSCHKO Management Group today. The result was that we could negotiate all of our contracts ourselves, ranging from those with our national and international TV partners to those with our service providers and sponsors. We also took on the ticketing, which is a very important factor when it comes to huge halls and even stadia.

The risks involved in setting up our own company were considerable because from then on we as the organizers had to shoulder the responsibility for organizing our events which involved many thousands of spectators. Yet I was never in any doubt that it had been the right step to get into the proverbial driver's seat and take control of the steering wheel. I keenly desired to be able to make independent and self-sufficient decisions together with my brother and Bernd Bönte.

In a certain sense I was afraid of what we were letting ourselves in for with this decision. It did not change things, though. Instead, it had the opposite effect: if you are afraid, you need to show courage and prove yourself. And I needed to move; I wanted a new challenge. Only cowards run away, put their heads in the sand or just let things carry on as before despite being dissatisfied. None of these three are good and none of them suit me either in business terms or in any other area of life.

I like the tingling in my fingers and my belly that critical situations give me. I make use of that adrenalin rush. Fear for me is an even better motivator than joy. Fear gives me a high when I realize that I am making the right choice. I want to do it. I square up to the challenge, accept it and master it. Under any circumstances.

That's what it was like then, too, and my persistence was rewarded: That same year the fitness chain McFIT, the commercial TV channel RTL, and Deutsche Telekom AG all became our partner brands. All of these were a perfect match for how we positioned ourselves.

Yet this was not the end of the journey for me. I wanted more.

With the KLITSCHKO Management Group we built a team and an organization that enabled me to pursue other ideas and initiate projects. I did not just need sparring partners inside the ring but also outside it; people to help me structure and organize myself. Over the years I have noticed that there are lots of people like me: they have the talent, but they are not well-structured. Athletes, in particular, fail to apply their knowledge away from the ring or playing field. Let's take Emanuel Steward as an example. He was my coach and an absolute guru in boxing, but unfortunately he was poorly structured and only ever passed his knowledge on 1-to-1, from coach to athlete. What a waste!

If he had passed on his knowledge in books, seminars or online, then thousands might have benefited from it. However, he passed away without having done this, which means that his immense wealth of experience has been lost.

I wanted to do things differently. My aim was to leave my mark and to pass on my knowledge. For this I needed more support. Tatjana Kiel, who has been by my side since 2006 as event and brand co-coordinator, shared my view that my vision might work. We therefore got started on my positioning and in "healthy aging" found a topic that we could credibly stand for. As sports scientists Vitali and I did not just have all the background knowledge about training and nutrition, but we had also applied this practically as athletes. Neither ageing nor health were seen positively in society as a whole at the time. I wanted to change this. In my eyes, our health is our most valuable possession.

Tatjana Kiel and I both liked the idea of building a brand that would last beyond the end of my sporting success and my boxing career. I was always surprised and scared by the fact that even the most successful athletes in the world seemed to spend little thought on what to do after their active time in their sport was over. It was almost as if they were amazed that their career was going to end at some point. Some turned their hand to becoming a coach or a TV pundit after they ended their professional careers. Others, however, seemed to be at a loss as to what to do with their lives. With just a few exceptions, this lethargy among top athletes has not changed much over the years. They spend their lives aimlessly wasting their money and many end up bankrupt.

I never wanted to suffer this sense of emptiness, which is why we started to ponder what "stage" there might be for me after the boxing ring. This was the starting point for developing initial strategies for my "career after my career", and we worked in parallel on discussions about my "career during my career" and on working out strategies for the guiding principle for my brand. For this we expanded the existing cores of my brand, namely "Brain", for mental strength, and "Power", for physical fitness.

But what did this mean? As a longtime professional boxer it was an obvious choice to stand for physical fitness. Deriving products and services from this aspect was entirely plausible. However, what would be the ideal way to position myself in terms of "Brain", to market mental strength and to enable others to profit from it?

I knew what my long-term goal was. I wanted to establish a management method in order to transfer my knowledge from the world of sport into the world of business. I was hoping to secure as a partner a top university with professors and institutes of note. However, I was still a long way from achieving this.

When it came to the method and contents with which we could establish the "Brain" sub-section, our answer was "Challenge Management". This topic cropped up while we were developing the "career after my career". Becoming a boxing manager was out of the question for me. My second stage was to be bigger, wider and more complex. I wanted to address several topics, initiate changes and work in different fields in parallel. For this we founded KLITSCHKO Ventures in 2016. In this company we bring together new business ideas and involvements that have only slight, if any, links with boxing.

From talking to managers and fans of boxing I knew that they were interested in my experiences and solutions. In their professional and private lives they faced ever new and ever more demanding challenges. For many years, companies had been initiating change processes every few years in order to keep up with the rest of the market. As a result of digitalization and globalization, nowadays one process after the other gets rolled out, with some even running in parallel. This complexity is too taxing for many people's working lives. They wish for a guide in order to find their way through the thicket of challenges they face.

Will they manage to find answers to all questions quickly enough and solve complex tasks by themselves? Probably not. However, we all can acquire the tools to deal confidently with challenges: to notice them in good time, assess them and master them; and to remain in the proverbial driver's seat despite the complexity. I myself often felt like I was stuck in a hamster wheel until I consciously decided to get out of it. Challenge Management helped me achieve this.

It seemed to us the right next step to introduce my approach to the decision-makers in business, associations and the administration. Then and now it was all about the methods that I developed based on my sport throughout the years.

My foundation stones for mastering challenges are mental strength and physical power. These are based on the four columns that have underpinned me in my sporting career for more than two decades: Focus, Agility, Coordination and Endurance. Having put these pillars of my success into words explicitly, I realized that these principles can be transferred virtually straight into the world of business: to be successful in our jobs, we also need Focus, Agility, Coordination and Endurance. It's just that in the business world they are called focus, flexibility, organization and stamina.

Finally I had got to where I wanted to be: I no longer just wanted my image to do the work, but I wanted actually to pass on real expertise. The only thing missing was actual products and services.

When we began to define a possible portfolio, I remembered a conversation I had had with Roger Jenkins, who was one of the most successful bankers in Great Britain at the time. Really, he was the first top manager who recognized the value I held for management. At the time I was considering whether I ought to gain an additional degree to consolidate my knowledge of the world of business. I was considering an MBA—a master's degree in business administration—from Harvard University.

I told him about my idea, but he was totally opposed to it: "If you do an MBA, you just lose time," he told me. "You already have so many qualities from your sport, so much practical knowledge that you carry within you. You just need to mine it".

In the beginning I did not understand what he meant. My upbringing had taught me that education was a valuable resource. It is the foundation on which we build our professional tasks. I was irritated by Jenkins' dismissing the MBA as a waste of time. To understand him better, I had a closer look at successful people and their résumés.

As a matter of fact I noticed that recognition, performance and sustainable success have little to do with someone's education background. I have met a great many clever people who lacked a can-do attitude; people who dared not and shied away from challenges. They were frequently surpassed and overtaken by capable, hands-on doers. I call the latter "street smart" people who have common sense, listen to their gut feeling and have courage.

This is the group I feel I belong to. I have a can-do attitude the same as many athletes, but which managers sometimes lack. They might be afraid of making mistakes. They might have forgotten, or maybe have never learnt, to listen to their gut feeling and have grown cowardly or have always been thus.

Over time therefore I started to understand my friend Roger Jenkins. I already had within me a great wealth of knowledge and experience. These I had long since developed into strategies. I did not need any further input in a particular area. Rather, I needed to find ways and means of mobilizing my know-how so that it could be me who was inspiring and educating students at a top business school.

This is how I found the solution: I was going to initiate a university course and teach "Challenge Management" in cooperation with a renowned university. The University of St. Gallen in Switzerland, as one of the top five business schools in Europe, was my first choice. Consequently, we started talks with the Institute for Customer Insights at St. Gallen in 2014. Happily we quickly found advocates within the university. We agreed to offer a CAS training course (Certificate of Advanced Studies) on the topic of "Challenge Management". We also quickly won the support of Professor Wolfgang Jenewein, one of the three heads of the institute and director of the "Executive MBA" program, an extra-occupational master's course for executives.

Unfortunately we had to postpone the start date by one year due to an injury and a delayed fight, but in February 2016 the time had come for us to be able to announce the commencement of our course: The University of St. Gallen and KLITSCHKO Ventures would work together in a long-term collaboration to deliver the course "CAS Change & Innovation Management". Under my leadership, professors of the university, who had been selected by Wolfgang Jenewein, as well as experts from the business world were to prepare executives optimally for dealing with professional and personal challenges.

Therefore we did not just need to gain the support of the university but also had to inspire experts from the business world to play an active role within the course. We considered especially carefully which managers or entrepreneurs had experience that fit with the contents of our course and that would add value if they were shared on a meta level. For this we drew on personal contacts, bounced ideas off trusted companions and listened to their recommendations. Eventually we managed to draw up a list of valuable experts. Convincing them and winning them over for our course was actually quite easy in the end—even though the course did not exist yet and they had never even heard of the field of study.

Frank Dopheide, Managing Director of Handelsblatt publishing group, became a long-term collaborator. As a real expert with regard to branding he had helped us with further developing the Klitschko brand and its marketing potentials. I was desperate to have him on board and was pleased when he agreed spontaneously on the phone.

It was a similar story with Jean-Remy von Matt, the founder of the renowned creative agency Jung von Matt, whom I had met in the mid-2000s while I was shooting an advert for the Milchschnitte brand. He is one of the few in the fast-paced advertising business who has managed to stay at the top for decades and has long since become a brand in his own right. I was therefore more than happy when he agreed, too. His topic: self-marketing.

Thus, we were working away, securing expert after expert until at the start of the course we had lined up, in addition to the university lecturers, seventeen experienced business practitioners to share their experiences and knowledge with the participants.

For the second year we rearranged the course contents slightly. I am very proud that thanks to those alterations we managed to secure as lecturers such renowned persons as, for example, the Global General Manager Platform and Innovation, Rolf Schumann, and the CEO of Deutsche Fußballliga (DFL), Christian Seifert.

My pride in this achievement is rooted in the fact that I still meet with suspicion from members of the business world. The good thing about this is: If people underestimate me then I can convince them of my expertise and my insights much faster.

"Wladimir Klitschko is known for having mastered new challenges for decades in timely and innovative ways", Jenewein said at our shared press conference on the occasion of the start of the course. "In the time of digitalization the future becomes ever harder to predict. The world becomes more volatile, insecure and complex. Against this background, we are pleased to be able to provide our executives with new impulses based on parallels from high-performance sports".

This presentation gained incredible interest in the media, but it also threw up questions: a boxer who initiates a university course? The journalists, one has to say, were rather skeptical. I, however, was able to convincingly outline for them my expertise and the strategy that resulted from it. Our collaboration with university professors and experienced managers also garnered positive attention. It was, in fact, absolutely unique to have both theoreticians as well as renowned practitioners preparing students to manage challenges.

There is one thing that particularly reassured me in our work: Even though I was not able to be there every day, "my" experts succeeded in making the participants during that first year feel as if I had indeed been there with them. They managed this by getting across the contents and experiences of Challenge Management using stories from our working together or personal anecdotes.

I myself do not lecture from the blackboard about what I teach, but make it real instead. During one so-called Challenge Evening the students thought up tasks to challenge me with. Some of these tasks really made me laugh but at the same time showed me that the students wanted to understand and get to know me better. We agreed a handful of tasks including a press-up competition and a stare down and ended up challenging each other. Stare down comes from the world of boxing where it is a custom for opponents to face each other before the fight and try to force down the other person's gaze. The evening was a huge success and I don't think any of us will ever forget it. We won, we lost, and we laughed a lot.

Just a few months after successfully completing the course, some of the graduates contacted me to let me know about incredible changes. Some had set up their own businesses; others had reached their desired position within the company; a new brand had been registered; several triathlons had been completed; and a lot of other ideas had been developed. One of the participants had even used his foundation to set up a scholarship for the next round of our course. He had been so impressed with it that he was determined to enable others to take part also.

When I heard "my" former students' stories, I was proud, moved and sometimes even overwhelmed. They really had faced their challenges head on. They moved forwards and became a moving force.

After completing the second round of the course I can definitely say: Challenge Management works. It is not rocket science; rather, it is a simple way of using new momentum to re-take control of your life.

As a consequence, we have expanded our collaboration with the university by setting up a Competence Center within the Institute for Customer Insights at the University of St. Gallen in summer 2016 to explore the methods and practices of "intrapreneurship". This term combines "intracorporate" and "entrepreneurship" and it signifies the entrepreneurial behavior of employees within an organization or company. The focus of the research is self-management and Challenge Management and the resulting question: How can we lead ourselves, motivate ourselves, stick with it and pick ourselves back up after being defeated?

The results of this research will back up my expertise even more. They will also be valuable insights that will not just become a part of the course but from which we can also derive other products in the future.

What a milestone for me as a professional boxer of many years!

Last year I was invited to speak at a conference which dealt with digitalization and the challenges it brings with it. As I got on the stage I could clearly see on the audience's faces in the front rows that they were happy to see a former world champion boxer in front of them but were wondering what I might have to say about digitalization. As always, this brought out my fighting spirit. I wanted to enthuse them and win them over to my way of thinking. I felt the challenge and wanted to show them: In front of you, you see not just got a boxer, you see a businessman, a founder, and a doer who has lots to tell.

It goes without saying that I was well-prepared. I met my 300 listeners, who included both managers and employees, as they were: hesitantly skeptical. I put their doubts into words—"What might the boxer be able to tell us?"—and told them about the parallels between them and me, namely that fear of digitalization and its consequences were comparable to my worries. How many jobs is digitalization going to cost, how many older or less educated people will be left behind? I ask myself a similar question in adapted form: Will my next opponent expose or provoke me? Will he defeat me because he is younger and fitter? And what will I do when I cannot box any longer?

The answer to these questions is simultaneously simple and complex: Everyone is in control of shaping their fortune. There are no problems, there are only challenges. However, we have to be prepared to recognize, evaluate and master them. If we do not manage this on one occasion, it does not necessarily equal defeat. Maybe we just need to change our goal. Or our path is taking a different turn than planned. We have it in our hands which challenge we choose to confront. It is not the end of the world if we make a mistake and it does not mean defeat. Only if we make the same mistake again or keep making it does it turn into foolishness. Every single person can be a moving force.

At this conference I clearly got through to my audience. The organizer extended the collaboration with us because he realized: A boxer can land punches outside the ring as well as inside.

Conclusion

- I am not interested in short-term goals.
- I want to be a competent, valuable and reliable partner for companies. I want expertise transfer, not image transfer.
- Challenge Management helps me successfully master the numerous challenges of my sport as well as my everyday working life.
- There are four pillars that support me in this: Focus, Agility, Coordination, and Endurance.
- I am happy to pass my experiences and insights on to others.

4. Knowledge Grows if We Share It

Over the years I have noticed that many people's problems are homemade. Often they view the smallest hurdles as insurmountable problems and mere difficulties as existential crises. For a while I wondered whether my life was really that much easier and freer of disruption than theirs. But then I realized that: it isn't; rather, it is all about how you look at things. The majority of people increasingly think in terms of problems. They frame everything in terms of a worst-case scenario—What could happen in the worst case?—and are governed by a passive and frightened way of thinking which means that they block their own actions.

I, on the other hand, prefer to look at solutions. If a challenge takes shape in front of me, I take it sportingly and see it as a test that needs mastering. " How do I get past this?" I ask myself. "How do I manage to just about get over this obstacle and how might I get over it significantly better than others?"

To answer this question I like to seek inspiration from people with experience. Whenever I get the chance I try to find out: "What was the biggest hurdle in your life? How did you master it?" It does not matter whether their experiences relate to my life or not: I can profit from any of the stories. Over time the way in which the anecdotes were told to me has given me a lot of insight into the narrators' attitudes. Some even seem out of their depth if I ask them my question. Maybe they think it unusual that I am interested in their lives.

These conversations made me aware that I do not think in terms of problems but challenges. I don't mean this to sound arrogant but self-confident in the best possible sense. In my life, too, there were periods when things were not going well. Yet I decided against just allowing myself to drift along. I myself make the decisions about where I am going.

Every defeat we suffer we can learn from. In anything bad we can also find something good, of this I am convinced. A defeat, in my view, is not a failure but an unexpected turn that life takes. We should always be ready to analyze our mistakes and to draw our conclusions from them so that the next time we can do better. This is how so-called defeats become successes.

This approach works both on the macro and the micro levels. Let us consider, for example, the human desire to innovate. At the end of the 19th century, the pioneering German aviator Otto Lilienthal would never have managed to complete a succession of gliding flights over a distance of 250 meters had he not failed numerous times previously just like many other brave hopefuls. His eventual success was possible only because he had viewed his previous failures as an incentive to improve rather than to give up.

We can transpose this same scenario into our time. Is it acceptable if self-driving cars cause accidents and people are injured? No, it is terrible. Injuries and, even worse, fatalities have to be avoided. Every death is one too many. Does this mean that the development of autonomous cars will be stopped? No, not under any circumstances. Because it is progress and will move humanity forward.

If I consider the micro level, using myself as an example, I think of my boxing defeats in 2003 and 2004. The defeats were bitter, and they led me to doubt myself. Yet, did I therefore feel like giving up and quitting boxing? No, never. Because I had a goal: I wanted to unite all important world champions' belts in our family with my brother Vitali. To achieve this I had to carry on.

It does not require witchcraft to move oneself from a passive, negative state of mind into an active, positive mood. We just have to make an active decision because no-one else can do this for us.

I have trialed this for years and intuitively developed a method of turning the problem into a challenge by following five steps. If you just move along from point to point, then you will find it easy to act in a solution-oriented fashion and to get out of the hamster wheel.

1. **Goal orientation:** Do you have a goal or are you drifting along? Define very precisely what it is you want to achieve.

2. **Consequences:** Draw up a worst-case scenario for yourself and imagine what will happen if you do not address your goal.

3. **Visualization:** Keep the best-case scenario in your mind's eye: Imagine you have already reached your goal. How does it feel? What are you doing?

4. **Companions:** Before you can get active, you need some comrades-in-arms: Who are your companions who will accompany you to your goal?

5. **Obsessiveness:** Think up at least one ritual and develop a plan of action so as not to lose sight of your goal. This way you can remember the vision of your best-case scenario every day. Love what you do.

I use this method in many situations: to prepare for an upcoming fight; or to find out what motivates a potential co-worker and to structure myself ahead of negotiations.

Let's have a look at them in order:

My Goal

Let us consider the boxing ring at the 1996 Olympic Summer Games in Atlanta. For years my vision, my grandest wish had been to be the first heavyweight boxer from the former Soviet Union to win an Olympic gold medal.

If I want to reach a goal, I need to be able to label it clearly and concisely. The more concrete, the better. The most important thing, however, is that I need to really want to achieve it. I need to be prepared to fight for it, otherwise I will give up at the smallest resistance.

Regarding the Olympics this meant: I wanted to win, not just take part. In my eyes, taking part would have been a "wishy-washy" goal that would have left too many backdoors open for me. I did not want to be able to say afterwards: "Well, bronze is good enough".

With managers I often notice that they are very good at formulating goals for their staff or the company, but they often forget about themselves. Or they follow goals not out of their own conviction or their own will, but because they might earn a bonus at the end. Against that background it is no surprise to me that some goals are only reached vaguely or not at all.

If I talk to executives about this dilemma, I like to tell them a harmless joke:

An old man dies and goes to heaven. When he gets to God, he tells him about his life. "I have been faithful all my life", he said. "Why did you never once let me win the lottery and make me rich?" he wanted to know. God frowned in confusion and answered: "For that you would have needed to play the lottery to begin with."

That is to mean: Make all your preparations and work towards your goal. Do not get tense; obstacles are there to regulate the course you are steering. Do not undertake too much at a time. Make sure also that the individual goals you have defined fit with your life goals and dreams.

Admittedly it is comparatively easy in sports to set yourself a big goal. In the world of business it sometimes appears much harder. If I need to get the overview in an inscrutable situation I think of what I know of the "Navy Seals", a US Special Forces unit. To set goals, everyone needs to have learnt to take aim properly beforehand. The Seals take aim at their target by not actually focusing on that target but on several points around it. They concentrate on the boundary points of the sight on their guns. The actual target they only perceive as a blur.

This way of proceeding seems to me a good blueprint for both job and everyday life. It helps us prioritize our goals. Without any pangs of guilt we can delete insignificant goals from our memory without losing sight of the next step. Let us do a practical exercise to demonstrate this: Think of your next big professional step. Keep it in the back of your head and note down 25 goals you need to be able to implement this step. Next, sort all these goals in hierarchical order (goal no. 1 = important, no. 25 = unimportant). Now cross out all goals from number six onwards. Not just on your piece of paper but also in your head. Should one of the crossed-out points show up in your thoughts from now on, shove it to the side consciously and without guilt. That way you can fully concentrate on what lies ahead of you.

Therefore: Do not act like the old man who spent his life dreaming of winning the lottery. Do not keep things vague. Put your goals, and your life goals too, into words and work at achieving them.

➡ If you want to evaluate or re-prioritize your goals, take a step back first and look at them from another level. The change of perspective will help to sharpen your focus.

The Consequences

Let's go back to the Olympic Games in 1996 where I was determined not to leave with anything other than a gold medal. Then as now I asked myself the following questions ahead of important decisions: What would happen if I did not reach the goal? How would it feel if everything stayed as it was before? How would it feel if I did not accept the challenge?

I mentally approach the situation with such intensity that when I just think of these questions I feel a cold chill running down my spine and I feel like I failed. This is the only way I can motivate myself to continue on to the goal, even if the path there is stony.

My opponent in the Olympic finals was to be Paea Wolfgramm, a guy from Tonga who weighs 130 kg. He was a colossus of a boxer. What, I asked myself, would happen if I did not beat him?

I would look like I did after my first few fights at the sports boarding school: black and blue in the face and covered with grazes and bloody wounds to such an extent that I would not recognize myself in the mirror. The pain would be terrible and for several days after it would hamper me and keep reminding me that I had taken on the challenge only half-heartedly.

I would be incredibly disappointed with myself, just as my brother, my family and my fans would be. Also, I would probably have to put off starting a career as a professional boxer. After all, a silver medal winner is not worth half as much as a golden boy.

I thought so intensely about these consequences that I could actually feel the discomfort. The terrible feeling of possibly being beaten up and to disappoint myself was an incredible driving force. I wanted to reach my goal. I wanted that gold medal.

➡ What will happen if you do not reach your goal? Think yourself into the situation intensely. Do not embellish anything and imagine the feeling that you get when you do not change anything. This discomfort is your driver for change.

The Visualization

I am a visual person. I am good at remembering faces. I recognize almost everyone who I had a longer conversation with over the last few years. Often I even still remember the environment in which the meeting took place. Their names, however, are a different issue entirely.

As a consequence, I use images to motivate me and to remind myself of my goal as easily as clicking my fingers. For example, I will see myself in a winning pose after an important fight, fists held high up in the air, a grin on my face and the cheering spectators in the background. This image is the first thing that comes to my mind in the morning and the last thing I think of at night.

Back then, in the summer of 1996, I went through this ritual, too. I even had a sort of film playing in my head: I remembered my fight at the Ukrainian youth heavyweight championship. I was 15 years old and had only just reached the minimum weight of 85 kilograms. My opponent in the finals was a strong athlete. André Klein his name was, I remember it clearly. We were sitting in our allotted corners before the fight began and he was sounding off because, unlike his name "Klein" suggested (which means "small" in German), he was anything but slight. At 120 kg he was a mountain of a man. "I'll never manage this", I thought. His body seemed unbelievably massive, and on top of this he was arrogant.

We were sitting in our allotted corners before the fight began, and he was boasting: "I'm going to finish that Klitschko. I'm going to knock him out in the first round ...." "Maybe you will knock me out," was my answer, "but definitely not in round one." I definitely wanted to get through three rounds, I decided.

Accordingly, I spent the beginning of the bout constantly dancing around in the ring, which gave my opponent hardly any chance of landing a hit. I got through the first round and called over to him from my corner: "See, you didn't manage." I was happy, and he was annoyed.

In the following round I did the same and noticed with surprise that André Klein was gasping, obviously he was already out of breath. In the third round I gathered up my courage and punched him. I would never have thought it possible, but I succeeded in knocking him out with a few well-aimed hits. He had boasted big time and over-estimated himself massively. And I managed to defeat André Klein, who was as huge as a bear.

These images always stayed in my mind after that. During the Olympic finals I used them to virtually program myself: In my mind I called on the images of the massive guy Klein and used them to motivate myself. I thought of this arrogant lump, whom I had defeated despite his weight. This gave me a real push that helped me to achieve the win against the 130-kg guy from Tonga.

➡ What image comes to your mind when you think of your success? Internalize your winning pose. Save similar motivational pictures on your smartphone and have a look at them if you have doubts. Social media platforms like Instagram or Pinterest are also a good source of inspiration.

The Companions

Before I begin to follow my goal, I need sparring partners, companions, and sometimes also experts. It does not matter whether I prepare for a boxing bout, initiate a project or present in front of a big audience: I seek out people who can help me improve. People who train with me, give me feedback, support me, or simply have the same goal. I am only good as part of a team, while as a lone warrior I do not get very far.

There is a maxim that I like to follow: "If you are the smartest person in the room, you are in the wrong room." This means that when I look for new staff I always try to find clever people. I am happy when I am surrounded by people who are smart and will enable me to get ahead.

It might seem strange that I see myself as a team player even though as a boxer I always have to confront my enemy on my own. Yet any sport is a team sport—no matter whether I stand on a pitch with some team mates or on my own in the ring. In elite sports it is impossible to reach one's goal without companions, partners and team colleagues.

In preparing for a fight, these people are my coach, my sparring partners in the ring, my physiotherapist, my chef as well as the staff who work away in the background, dealing with the marketing, negotiating contracts or managing press relations. This might sound inconsequential, but it is not. Every single one of these people contributes to my being successful and being able to concentrate on the essentials. They are all aware that I need their full support in order to reach the goal.

Sometimes it is even an opponent who leads me towards my goal. This is not due to their being especially easy to defeat, but because they motivate me to change my preparation regime or provide me with some other impulse.

This means: Companions do not necessarily have to pull in the same direction, but they contribute in one way or another to my achieving what I have set out to achieve.

→ You need companions to reach your goal better, faster, more securely and with more motivation. Make a list of possible companions: Who stands for what motives and interests? Only agree to cooperations if they are profitable for both sides.

Obsessiveness

Without perseverance no-one will remain successful in the long term. Yet stamina on its own does not suffice for achieving outstanding successes.

If you want to excel, you need passion. I have to have a burning passion for my sport, my job, and my ideas in order to be one of the best in the long term. I need obsessiveness.

I find it interesting that this term has a negative connotation. Obsessiveness has a tinge of doggedness with a touch of frenzy and madness. Yet for me obsessiveness means the love of the goal.

It is obsession that drives sportspeople to top performances and artists to creative masterpieces.

I love what I do, otherwise I would never have managed to keep going for this long. It is wonderful when I follow a goal and periodically work at it as if in a frenzy. I have not just experienced this during my training camps or on other occasions as an athlete. I also know it as a businessman when I fine-tune a strategy with my team or we shut ourselves away to create something totally new in a mutual exchange of ideas.

Obsessiveness is a sustained fascination that does not allow for excuses or apologies of any kind. I see it as a grand engine that drives me with incredible force. This is another reason why it is important for me personally and for us as a team to define big and long-term goals. No-one ever manages to be passionate about micro goals, let along burn with enthusiasm.

How, then, do I manage to develop obsessiveness? How do I succeed in loving my goal? How do I sharpen my senses for it? The prerequisite is that I identify myself with what I do; that I like it. I should continuously bring to mind that I have consciously decided to take on my challenge. There are five criteria that make me obsessive:

1. "Always stay in motion": As soon as I have identified my goal, I set off towards it, straight toward the finish line. Being indecisive means losing one's sense of orientation. It means that the temptation to stop moving forward increases. Yet, stopping is the same as moving backwards. I learnt this from my father and his military environment. As we all know, an army is drilled to march straight ahead towards the goal during missions. It may well be that the fear inside their heads is shouting at them to turn and run away, but giving in to this needs to be avoided at any cost.

Oliver Wurm, a media entrepreneur and one of the lecturers at St. Gallen, has a different perspective on things than I do, yet reaches the same conclusion. "Even if you fall flat on your face you are moving forward", he says. The truth within this is that when things go wrong it does not necessarily signify defeat. Maybe it quite simply brings about a change of direction.

2. **"Pain is fear leaving your body"**: "Pain is fear leaving your body" is another motto from the military. It implies that we ought to endure a certain level of pain because it makes us stronger and fit for greater challenges.

If the challenge is particularly big then there is no shame in being afraid. On the contrary: Fear is healthy because it mobilizes us. Only being cowardly is unforgivable because it makes us lose control.

There is another undercurrent in this soldiering maxim: If I feel pain, then I know I am still alive despite being wounded.

In sport or our everyday working lives there obviously are few parallels to injuries like that. Yet the maxim is still valid. It tells us that we need to conquer negative feelings, maybe even fear, to reach our goal. If we have mastered something unpleasant and were not scared off by it then we will be stronger next time and will reach our goal more easily.

3. **"Resistance"**: During the good times I prepare for the bad. Because one thing is certain: whatever route I take towards my goal, I will experience resistance along the way, either from myself or from the outside world.

It is essential that I make myself aware of this in advance. If I am prepared for it, then I am ready. Obstacles and hurdles will not be able to knock me over; instead they will just make me rethink my path and maybe adapt it. A healthy level of egotism supports me in this respect. This is because only by thinking of myself and by feeling good about the situation will I have the assertiveness to overcome obstacles.

4. **"Be multidimensional, not one-dimensional"**: There are many paths to a goal, and no two paths are the same. In any given situation, I try not to think in black and white terms, but to see and understand the points of view of all parties involved. If, for example, I am working with partners, then I always want to understand their views and reasons. If we agree to share the same path for a while to reach a common goal, then I am only

prepared to do so if our approaches complement each other. Synergies should arise that benefit both sides. If in the end there is no solution that is actually better, then I would rather forego the cooperation.

5. "Do your homework": To be able really to throw myself into a project, I have to be sure that I am investing my energy and passion wisely. Anything else would mean throwing myself into it without using my head, but this is not the same as working obsessively. Therefore it is important to me that I think through the significance and meaning of my project and to analyze its impact before I get started.

In the run-up to a boxing bout this is especially important. When, for example, I competed against Anthony Joshua in spring 2017, there was an especially wide range of topics to cover. With an audience of 90,000, interest was already immense well before the fight. We drew up a plan of action to make sure all topics got dealt with. What date should we choose? How should we plan the media appearances? How should my training be organized? What sparring partners ought we to choose? What should the nutrition schedule look like? What hotel should we stay in? There were a thousand questions that all needed to be addressed so that I could focus my full attention on the physical preparation; so that I was able to work obsessively towards my goal.

To be successful in the long term it is essential that I preserve moments of success and draw upon them almost as part of a ritual. Images of success—as described in the section "Visualization"—help me get into a positive and motivated mood. It goes without saying that even I do not feel obsession, a sustained sense of enthusiasm, in every second of my life. Yet when I put my boots on at the start of my training and am still feeling a bit off-color or tired maybe, I recall these meaningful images in my mind. They give me a real sense of what it means to be an Olympic winner and how great it feels to reach my ambitious goals, and this gives me the kick I need to begin training. Confidently at the start, and more and more obsessively as time progresses.

➡ Look for tasks and goals that you are enthusiastic about. This will help you keep at it even when times get tough. Be prepared for the fact that obstacles may arise. Consider them an aid for finding the right path towards your goal.

For all of those who feel that this five-step method only works for sports, I would like to give the following example: Since we started building an organization for my "career after my career", we have been needing reinforcement staff in various areas.

When I was in the process of finding a manager for a new unit, I kept my five steps in my mind during every interview I conducted. They helped me in choosing the perfect candidate for the vacancy:

1. Goal: Every candidate's goal had to be to get the job and to turn the business idea into an achievable, marketable concept.

My question to them was therefore: "How will you achieve this goal? And what would you like to implement by this both professionally and in your private life? Why is this goal important to you?"

The various answers demonstrated clearly how the applicants' thought processes worked, how they would approach their task, and what ideas they had for filling the job with life.

I expect my staff to have a burning passion for their job and to do anything to reach the desired goal. If during the interview I read between the lines that this job is just one option among many, I lose interest in the candidate. Frequently I end the interview there and then because I realize: this candidate would need to be motivated by me constantly in order to reach our goals. That, however, would demotivate me in the long run.

2. Consequences: What would happen if the candidate did not get the job? What would the candidates be prepared to give for their job and what would happen if we turned them down? Also, what would happen if they got the job but did not reach the intended goal?

Do they want this job because it sounded quite interesting or would it be a catastrophe for them to miss this chance?

I expect the candidates to demonstrate to me in how far they are prepared to suffer and how much they want to get the job. If they answer that it is of no consequence if they do not get the job, then they are of no interest to me. In that case the applicant is no candidate.

3. Visualization: I asked them what image they imagine of the moment when they, or rather we, reach our goal. What would our launch or opening party look like, what success did they visualize?

This showed me: How big were they thinking? What visions did they have? How innovative were they? How many question marks were hanging over them and how risk-taking or risk-averse did they show themselves to be?

4. Companions: Which people are necessary to best push our business idea? Who are the obvious supporters and who might be useful even though it may not seem obvious at first sight?

I asked the candidates: What contacts would you be able to bring to the company? Which companions could you secure as a matter of urgency? And how would they react if they found that the ideal companions would be their former competitors or even enemies?

The answers showed me clearly who was loyal and honest. As most applicants do not expect questions like these, they answer either very reservedly or very honestly. I have a sixth sense for that detecting reactions like these.

5. Obsessiveness: I need staff who are in full agreement with their job, their ideas and our vision and who throw themselves fully into their work. This does not mean I want them to work day and night, of course. They should be able to recognize hot project phases as such and then bring all their passion and creativity to bear on them. My staff should identify themselves with their task. It is important to me that everyone knows, understands, and feels what their place in the team is.

Consequently, I asked the applicants this simple question: "How much do you want this job?" Was there a comparable task that they were prepared to do?

And finally: Could they imagine subordinating everything else to this task for the first few months?

There is joke that fits with this, which I occasionally tell applicants:

Communist Party ideologists are conducting an interview with a candidate to establish how firm his convictions are.

They ask him: "Are you prepared to give up smoking for the good of the Communist Party?"

The candidate answers: "Oh, I love smoking! That will be hard. But okay, I will give it up for the Party."

The communist comrades continue: "Are you prepared to give up drinking for the good of the Party?"

He is taken aback by this: "Oh dear, drinking is my favorite vice ... Well, okay, I will give it up for the Party."

The communists then ask a third question: "Are you prepared to live in celibacy and to renounce sex for the Party?"

The candidate is appalled: "What? What are you asking of me? This is inhumane. But okay, if that is the condition, then I will live in celibacy for the Party."

At last the communists ask him: "Would you be prepared to give your life for the Party?"

The candidate answers without missing a beat: "Yeah, sure."

The communists are surprised. "Why did you agree so quickly this time?"

"It's obvious, isn't it?", says the candidate. "Life's no fun anyway without smoking, drinking and sex."

It's a silly little story, but with a little twinkle in the eye it gets across that I demand enthusiasm from my staff. Candidates who understand this laugh about the joke and some may add that they would like to hang on to their vices if possible please. Applicants who think differently, however, often look reserved and more than a little disconcerted when I tell this little story.

Conclusion

- The way in which I meet life's challenges determines the outcomes that I achieve.
- If I go about tasks in a passive and frightened way then I block my own actions.
- If I view obstacles like a sporting exercise, then the likelihood of my overcoming them is higher.
- In five steps I manage to turn a problem into a challenge.

Part II

My Twelve Ways to Respond to Challenges

Every problem is unique. Every obstacle, every resistance and every solution arise from a specific situation. I have noticed, however, that the patterns of the challenges repeat themselves, be it at work or in everyday life. I have found answers to these fundamentally similar situations and identified twelve ways in which I respond practically to the challenges. My solutions have their basis in sport, but have long since proved themselves in the world of business.

Enabling and Using Coopetition

Coopetition is the combination of cooperation and competition. The idea behind coopetition is that not just cooperative partners but also competitors work together and profit from this collaboration. The driver behind the coopetition may be the desire to save resources and to be environmentally friendly. The motivation may also be the desire to share know-how and experience in order to strengthen one's own position. Even dominant players nowadays lack the capacities or competencies to implement trends and innovations as quickly as possible all by themselves.

My Experience as an Athlete

Boxing could be considered a hotbed of coopetition. As I am an open and flexible person the idea of cooperative competition very much appeals to me. I am convinced that I can only improve if I open myself towards others, for example towards competitors and rivals. As a teacher I learn at least as much as my pupil. When preparing for a fight, I always train with sparring partners who may later become my opponents. This was the case, for instance, in April 2017 when I competed against Anthony Joshua in London. He had trained with me in 2014 while I was preparing for my bout against Kubrat Pulew.

I often provide my sparring partners with practical advice and even give them an insight into my training schedule. Some even got to wear my boxing boots, which I developed myself due to my dissatisfaction with the commercially available products. Years ago I had sat down with boxing boot specialists, had prototypes made and worked on the designs until I had the perfect boxing boot in front of me. Instead of viewing this boot as a means of gaining a competitive advantage and keeping it secret, however, I offer my sparring partners the opportunity to obtain similar custom-made boots.

My Experience as a Businessman

Cooperative competition also occurs elsewhere in the boxing environment. Promoters are competitors on the one hand, competing for the best sportspeople. On the other hand, however, they need to work together when it comes to matchmaking a fight. Both share an interest in putting on a good bout that as many fans as possible will want to watch and that attracts a lot interest from the media. Both sides separately are out to make the best deal for themselves, but this is not mutually exclusive.

Trends in the Business World

The case of the car industry demonstrates what happens when companies that are spoilt by their successes refuse to open themselves up. Competitors from outside the industry end up giving them a run for their money—whether this be by developing electric cars (Tesla) or self-driving cars (Google). By now, this has made even companies like VW, BMW, and Mercedes rethink. On one occasion they have joined forces with competitors to acquire the map service "Nokia Here" and use this for the navigation systems in their cars. On another occasion they have issued a joint invitation to a car summit to demonstrate the strength of their industry (see also the chapter Coopetition by Frank Dopheide in Part III).

Thinking Progressively and Acting Courageously

Although the theory might sound simple, it is often difficult to put into practice. If you want to create something new, you need to break free from convention, throw out your previous assumptions and change your perspective, and you must not allow yourself to be held back by doubters.

My Experience as an Athlete

I have never cared when other people told me: "That won't work. We've never done it that way." For example, I went against usual industry practice when I decided I was absolutely not going to choose a German pseudonym for my career as a boxer. Walter and Willi Klitschmann were the names that were suggested to Vitali and me at the start of our professional career in the mid-1990s. We turned this suggestion down politely. It was not just that we did not like those names but also that we felt it was more authentic and honest to compete under our real names.

My inclination is to question established practices and to think progressively and act courageously instead, both in the small and the bigger aspects of life. When I ponder where this tendency comes from, I am reminded of my grandmother and a story she told me that impressed me as a child:

When she was young, she worked at a restaurant where most of the customers were military men. Times were bad, the menu was limited, and the facilities were terrible. One day a high-ranking Communist found a cockroach in his meal. He furiously ordered the owner of the restaurant over to his table. The owner was shaking with fear as he worried that this influential guest would have his restaurant shut down. My grandmother was frightened too, but she put on a brave face, walked over to the table, grabbed the cockroach and swallowed it quickly. Then she told the soldier with a winning smile: "I am so sorry that you were served burnt onion." The guest was speechless at first and then pacified. The owner was utterly relieved, and my grandma got a bonus from her boss to reward her initiative. Courage pays.

My Experience as a Businessman

I enjoy taking the initiative, going down new paths and trying what no-one has tried before. Being a sportsman and becoming my own promoter? I've done that, and successfully so. A boxer setting up a course at a top business university? I've achieved that. And in addition, researching a management discipline that will motivate others? I'm doing that right now.

Trends in the Business World

For companies that have the courage to try something totally new there are two possibilities: to fail spectacularly or to become a positive example. The latter happened with the cosmetics business Dove. They ran an advertising campaign using normal women, whose bodies featured common problem zones and were not in line with usual beauty standards. Although there were some who raised concerns, those in charge of the campaign continued with the project and were rewarded by its success. Sales rose significantly, and Dove triggered a public discussion about the image of women, which inspired other producers, initiatives, and especially women themselves.

Learning from Defeats to Create New Potential

We often feel like losers if we have failed at something—whether this be vying for a contract, competing over a potential employee, or negotiating a pay rise. However, this way of looking at things actually is not beneficial as it does not help us do it better and be more successful next time.

My Experience as an Athlete

I can count on one hand the defeats I had to suffer as a professional boxer. Two of them had huge significance for my future career: losing against Lamon Brewster in fall 2004 and against Tyson Fury eleven years later. Each defeat was an enormous disappointment for me. Yet they also spurred me on to keep working at myself and improving. The first time round, I completely changed everything around that I had been doing up until then. I hired a new coach, found a chef and signed a new physiotherapist, to name just a few of those changes. The result proved me right: for years I won every fight.

In 2015, after being defeated by Fury, I also examined those responsible within my team but stuck with them. There was nothing I could blame them for in what had happened. Instead, I changed a lot of smaller details, such as redefining the rules in the training camp. Since then, I have been incommunicado to everyone for eight weeks before the fight, and I delegate everything outside my training to my team.

My Experience as a Businessman

As a businessman I act in a similar manner. If I fall flat on my face with an investment, then I analyze the causes, draw my conclusions and decide what further steps to take. It is only human to make mistakes. Yet to make the same mistake twice or more is akin to stupidity. When I was investing in an online shop together with a partner in the early days of the internet hype, I soon withdrew from it again. I realized that high amounts of investment, a lot of know-how and speed would be needed in order to have the chance to compete against the big beasts of the sector. I therefore decided not to pump any more money into it. I lost what I had already invested, but the loss was modest. I learnt my lesson from this: nowadays I analyze the market and its determining factors better and talk to people with expert knowledge before I decide to engage in an endeavor.

Trends in the Business World

Very slowly the realization that defeats can have positive implications seems to be gaining ground. At so-called fuckup nights failed business founders talk about their experiences to large audiences. In companies, too, there is recognition that mistakes can lead to successes. Let us have a look at the Danish toy manufacturer Lego. In 2004 Lego was fighting for its survival. With its merchandising sets for Harry Potter and other movies the company had strayed a long way from its core brand. Lego analyzed its errors, corrected its course and, for example, expanded its segment aimed at girls. Since then, the company has been sitting pretty again. Because Lego learnt from its previous wrong decisions and drew the right conclusions from them.

Making Use of Your Successes and Letting Others Partake in Them

Those who are successful should give back to society so that society can grow. This idea is one of the basic principles of a social market economy.

My Experience as an Athlete

"Fight for your dreams," is what I tell all young people who are unsure and let themselves be discouraged. Sometimes I actually mean this literally. Several years ago Vitali and I founded the "KLITSCHKO Foundation". Through this foundation we want to give back to society. Its aim is to support children and young people from disadvantaged families in Ukraine. By means of sports and educational projects we encourage them to assert themselves in their lives. We even chose "Fight for your dream!" as our motto.

My Experience as a Businessman

A few years ago I noticed during my swimming practice that I got out of breath quickly even though I felt fit all in all. I watched some other swimmers practicing for a competition and they obviously did not have the same problem with stamina that I had. They recommended to me that I should work with a "Power Breath", which trains the muscles involved in breathing and thus increases lung capacity. It is a simple piece of equipment; a kind of snorkel that expands lung volume, enabling more stamina and better concentration. I bought one of them and was thrilled, but at the same time I spontaneously felt that I could get more out of it still. I puttered about with it, cut off a bit of the tube somewhere and stuck it on someplace else until I found it perfect to use.

The commercially available products had obviously not been developed by athletes. The equipment was just impractical. Either it was too large to take along or it did not have the right resistance when breathing in and out. In the end I developed my own lung trainer, with which I am extremely satisfied. Compared to my previous lengths swum during training I improved my stamina by an estimated 40 percent.

Having used this product myself for years, I now want to make it available to others. I have improved it year after year and am therefore convinced that what I have to offer is in fact the best lung trainer on the market. I want others, whether sport is just their hobby or whether they are professionals, to be able to increase and improve their performance.

Trends in the Business World

In Germany the "Mittelstand", the small and medium-sized companies, have traditionally been known to support individuals, institutions, and communities near their sites. Sometimes this takes the form of financial aid, sometimes outreach work by their employees. From the USA an additional trend has arrived that enables new whiz kids also to become benefactors. The search engine company Google, for example, invests one percent of its corporate profits in charitable projects. The founder of Facebook, Mark Zuckerberg, and his wife have transferred 99 percent of their shares in a foundation. And through "The Giving Pledge," extremely wealthy individuals, among them Bill Gates, pledge to donate at least half their fortune to charity.

Planning Long-Term and Continuously Demonstrating Performance

If you want success, you need visions and goals—coupled with stamina.

My Experience as an Athlete

My job requires a very particular kind of time planning. In the last fifteen years I have competed on average two to four times per year. This constitutes the highest possible load every year: going through eight weeks of training camp at least twice a year; the chance to leave the ring as winner each time. But that was not enough. After all, I could not just spend the rest of the time leaning back and leaving sport be. I had to work long term towards the next bout, the next year, and continuously demonstrate performance; motivate myself constantly. I managed because I set big goals for myself and went about them with perseverance, discipline and patience.

My Experience as a Businessman

The development of "my career after the career" arose from my desire to plan long term. The fact that I was able to let both of these careers—as a boxer and an entrepreneur—run in parallel for several years was due to my team and myself continuously demonstrating performance. If I search for the origins of my discipline and perseverance, I am yet again reminded of my grandmother. When I used to sit over my homework at her house and groan about the amount of content to cover, especially in math, she reacted in an exemplary fashion. She did not tell me off for being unmotivated, but neither did she try to play down the work. She stressed how important it is to stick with: "Do 20 minutes of math, then another subject, and then math again." Sticking with it by means of variety was my grandmother's approach to all aspects of life. Today, this is what I pass on to my staff and colleagues.

Trends in the Business World

Businesses owe it to their staff and shareholders to plan long-term. Without vision and strategy the employees would not know why they should go to work and constantly perform well day in, day out. A look at different companies shows that there is huge variability in how such long-term plans can be phrased. Siemens, for example, wants to grow faster than its five main competitors thanks to its "Vision 2020". In 2010 the car company Audi formulated the goal in its "Strategy 2020" that they wanted to become the worldwide leader in the premium sector. And screw producer Würth uses figures to define its goal: having achieved sales of 5 billion euros in 2000, in the year 2020 the company wants to grow this to 20 billion euros.

Using Rest Periods to Reflect

Successful executives are good at many things: they are assertive, think strategically, are able to motivate others, and keep calm in turbulent times. What many of them need some extra help with, though, is relaxation.

My Experience as an Athlete

As a top athlete I learnt that tense periods absolutely have to be followed by a period of reflection. Without relaxation, there is no tension; without tension, there is no relaxation. I need eight weeks to get myself mentally and physically fit before a fight. To come down from this again afterwards only takes me a few days. During those days I do not do anything either physically or mentally, I power everything down and just relax. A little while after that I analyze my performance. I think about what possible conclusions I may be able to draw from it and about how to initiate improvements.

My Experience as a Businessman

Business successes for me serves as an occasion to pause for a moment. After a significant phase has been completed successfully, I like to get my team together to celebrate the moment and relish what we have achieved. I do not, however, just leave moments like these hanging in the air: a few days later I meet up with the same team members to evaluate what has been achieved and to discuss next steps.

I like to facilitate time out and reflection on an individual basis, too. If my staff reach their agreed goals then I will, for example, support them in their sports activities. If they can show that they attend fitness classes regularly, the company will sponsor their membership.

Trends in the Business World

In the fight for the best talent some employers began a long time ago to provide time out for their staff. These employers appreciate that pauses are essential for people achieving their potential. Large business consultancies, for example, are among the trailblazers and enable their employees to take sabbaticals without lots of paperwork and without embarrassment—regardless of whether the reason is a PhD, parental leave or a trip around the world. Corporations like Linde or Microsoft release employees for them to be able to volunteer for social schemes or other projects. Microsoft runs a volunteering program called "3 Days Off", which offers their staff three extra days in addition to their annual leave. Linde allows the workforce in some regions to take time out for private projects or for further training.

Focusing on the Essentials

The world is full of possibilities, and digitalization and globalization seem to provide a wealth of business opportunities. Yet this view can be fatal: If you try to use too many opportunities at once, you run the risk of getting bogged down and not achieving anything in the end.

My Experience as an Athlete

I have remained faithful to the above maxim ever since the start of my professional career. I always wanted to become world champion. Later, my goal was to keep the title and I focused on that. This becomes obvious at the training camp because there I expect the same level of focus from everyone around me. To paraphrase the "Golden Rules" formulated specifically for training camp: "Wladimir's success is the ultimate goal. Everything else needs to be subordinated to this, including personal feelings and issues." Routine helps me concentrate on what is most important. At training camp, therefore, every day is structured largely along the same schedule: getting up, training, breakfast, training, lunch and sleep, followed by boxing training and dinner. Anyone who arrives late has to pay a 150 dollar penalty and do 100 push-ups. The aim of this is to make everyone focus on the purpose of the camp: my victory.

My Experience as a Businessman

Happily, my companies and involvements are growing, which is why I delegate tasks and responsibilities to leading executives. To ensure that they all know my priorities and my ideas of what matters, we have come up with seven values that we use to develop products and services and base decisions on: expertise, rightness, globalism, optimism, sustainability, uncomplexity, maximum (see also the chapter Ergo Sum). These values help me not to get bogged down, and they provide direction for everyone in our group.

Trends in the Business World

One-product companies never fall out of fashion. Their brands are things such as Flexi (a dog leash), Bionade (a carbonated herbal drink), Jägermeister (a herbal liqueur), or Freitag (a courier bag), and their big advantage is that there is no way they could get bogged down. These companies invest their full concentration, their whole capacity and all their resources in just one single product. This almost entirely precludes any danger of errors being made through carelessness or inattention. The prerequisite for one-product companies to thrive is that they constantly check their USP: Does the product really stand a chance of occupying a leading position in the market? Is it strong enough to be able to carry a whole business? If the answer to these questions is "yes" then there is nothing to stop them from being successful.

Trusting Your Own Competences

"Horses for courses", an old proverb says. It only partially gets across what it means to trust in your own competences: to know your strengths, to use them and allow them to unfold beyond the same old routine. Employ them to the best effect.

My Experience as an Athlete

To trust in my own competences to me means to know my body and my mind, to care for them and count on them. Besides my fitness this also entails eating a balanced diet, sleeping well, and doing regular mental training.

For many years now I have been actively co-developing my training routines building upon my own experience, because I consider this very important. While other boxers prefer just to be told what to do, I have my own intuition that I value highly. My coach Johnathon Banks used to be a sparring partner of mine. He holds the proverbial mirror up to me and perfectly analyzes my actions. In this way we both influence my training schedules. In boxing this is rather unusual. Even my brother Vitali rarely used to get involved in how the preparation was to be set up.

My Experience as a Businessman

I know my strengths and put full trust in my competences. It is them that led me to develop the boxing boots and the lung trainer that I am going to bring to the market soon. This is why I initiated the executive training course at the University of St. Gallen and even expanded it with a designated competence center. My trust in my own competences is one of the reasons why I split from my promoter all those years ago in order to handle the marketing of my fights and of my own brand by myself. On such occasions, there are of course always people who question my decisions. Yet, when I know what I am capable of, I can meet incredulity and criticism with calm composure.

Trends in the Business World

Such composure can also be found in the business world. Smart, the company making subcompact cars, is moving around the world of SUVs and limousines without feeling in any way inferior. This is because its makers know exactly where the competences of this vehicle lie. The Smart is not small, they say, it is agile and fits into any car parking space. It is not slow but economical; not unsuitable for long distances but a perfect city car. Due to these competences and the according positioning, these little cars have long become an integral part of our cityscapes.

Way 9
Identifying Potential and Harnessing It

What potential is hiding in people, products and organizations that is still waiting to be discovered? Where are the potentials that aren't being used yet? And where do the strengths actually lie in totally different areas than we would have thought? Some people succeed in their endeavors without looking like they are even trying. Others fail at the simplest tasks because they misjudge themselves. Therefore, it is helpful to analyze one's strengths and weaknesses sensibly and deal with them honestly in order to identify and harness real potential.

My Experience as an Athlete

"Everybody is good at something. See it, use it, don't kill it all at once", is what I believe in. Over the years I have acquired a certain understanding of human nature. After all, it is part and parcel of my job to study my opponent as best possible before the fight, evaluate him in the ring and then to act accordingly.

Thus, I chose as my coach one of my former sparring partners. After my previous coach had died unexpectedly, I urgently needed a new one. My next fight was imminent. I had known Johnathon Banks for years. We had often trained together; I knew his abilities and his outstanding analytical skills. There were some who advised me against signing him, but I was not deterred. We have now been a team for five years.

I came by my physiotherapist in a similar way. Aldo Vetere was only 21 and had just finished his professional training when I met him. In his field, experience is usually considered key. Most physiotherapists working with top athletes have decades of practical experience. Yet I recognized Aldo Vetere's talent and his passion for his job. I therefore asked him to work for me. Now I cannot even imagine a camp without him.

My Experience as a Businessman

My feel for people also helps me as an entrepreneur. It aids me in choosing business partners just as much as in leading my staff. Sometimes it is even useful in giving career advice as this anecdote shows: A friend of mine, who is employed as a manager, is what I consider a born entrepreneur. For a long time he would not hear about it. Finally, on a yachting trip I agreed the following with him: If he dared jump off a railing with me, he would resign and set up his own business. I went first, and he found the courage to jump after me. Nowadays he is a much happier person and a successful entrepreneur.

Trends in the Business World

Although there were already dozens of vacuum cleaner brands on the market, the British inventor James Dyson spotted the potential for a new product: a bagless vacuum cleaner. The idea proved a success, and Dyson went on to develop other appliances that work by sucking up and blowing out air: a hand drier as well as a fan without blades. From a consumer's point of view these products have very little to do with each other, as cleaning, drying, and cooling are very different activities. From a producer's point of view, however, Dyson realized the full potential of air flows and used this shrewdly.

Explosively Releasing Top Performance

For top athletes this ability is essential: if you are at the top of your game in training, but cannot release the same level of performance in the real bout, you will never be a success. For businesses and executives, too, this ability is becoming increasingly important.

My Experience as an Athlete

During the many years I have spent on my boxing career, I have found a good way to prepare for a bout. This may be a bit of a surprise for outsiders, but the mental pressure is enormous before such an event with millions of spectators across the TV audience and in the arena. In addition to this, I also have to be 100 percent fit physically to stand a chance to win.

I prescribe myself eight weeks of training camp before each fight. In the last week before the fight, I reduce the training to a maximum of one hour per day and focus on mental training the rest of the time. Coming to rest, jettisoning unnecessary ballast, reminding myself of my strengths ... My experience has shown me that this is the best preparation I can do in order to be able to release top performance on the fight night; to confront my opponent in the ring with power, fast reactions and speed. I have, after all, no more than twelve rounds of three minutes each, during which I have to show what I am capable of.

My Experience as a Businessman

In the runup to an important presentation or negotiation I prepare meticulously. When the first lecture of our executive course in St. Gallen had to be prepared, my team and I spent days on the presentation. We compiled the contents, talked about the teaching method and discussed how to visualize it on the slides. Afterwards I practiced the presentation several times, always in front of someone unfamiliar with the topic. For the actual presentation I arrived a day early. 20 minutes before such appearances I always seclude myself, do not answer my phone and am not available for anyone to talk to. After committing the core messages fresh to my memory one last time, I am motivated with every fiber of my being and ready to give a top performance. Wherever I get the chance I use loud music to get myself in the mood—just like I do during boxing with the walk-in song *Can't stop* ...

Trends in the Business World

Red Bull is a master at ad-hoc performance shows: Their daredevil sky-diving events have grown to become well-known throughout the word and attract large numbers of spectators. On occasion they are staged without prior warning. In situations like those it is essential that companies have built up appropriate structures and deployed the right staff to ensure that such spontaneous, large-scale events work.

Creating Organizational Structures

In a small team it can be difficult to introduce clear structures and clearly assign responsibilities because the staffing level is so low. Similarly in large companies there is a danger that such clearly assigned responsibilities and hierarchies might smother their employees' empowerment.

My Experience as an Athlete

For the training camp we have defined clear structures and strict rules that apply to everyone involved. These parameters do not make any allowances and clearly set out responsibilities as well as liberties and boundaries. All staff members and sportspeople there work towards the goal of me winning the bout. My camp manager—who doubles up as my chef—is the point of contact for all organizational matters at the training camp. All sparring partners and their coaches are advised not to address their issues to me if at all possible. While this hierarchy is very much in evidence during training, it quickly dissolves into communal togetherness afterwards. Getting together as equals, I like to discuss strengths and weaknesses and consider whether tasks may need to be re-assigned.

My Experience as a Businessman

As I started off as a boxer and not a businessman, it took a while for us to organize my business activities into a unified structure. By now, such diverse enterprises as K2 Promotions, KMG, the design hotel 11 Mirrors, and KLITSCHKO Ventures have been brought together in one worldwide strategic group and share a unified umbrella brand. I am not interested in purely financial investments, but in passing on my experiences. The new organizational structure is providing the opportunity to steer the companies and create synergies.

Trends in the Business World

Many software boutiques and creative companies have dropped strict hierarchical forms of organization. One software producer in Hamburg, for example, makes do without any hierarchical levels at all. In order to give as much responsibility as possible to each employee and not just to select executives there are no job descriptions, no departments, no line managers, and no top-down structures. Essentially, this tech company is organized along the lines of one big project. This is meant to eliminate complexity and to minimize administrative effort.

The Berlin-based innovation agency Dark Horse also manages without any hierarchy. It is run by 30 founders, who all have totally equal rights. At Ministry, a communications agency, the teams are all on an equal footing. The founders consciously decided against setting up additional levels of hierarchy as the company grew. Instead, they passed on the right to make decisions to the individual units. These have full control over their working hours, vacations, customers, and marketing pitches.

Established companies are on the back foot in this respect. Their organizational structure, including their hierarchies and decision-making processes, are long-established. To re-invent them can be a very slow process. Some firms, for example RWE and E.ON, have therefore taken the route of setting up successor companies, in which they can define entirely new rules.

Knowing and Using Your Opponent's Strengths and Weaknesses

In the world of work there are few people who are as tuned into analyzing their opponents as sportspeople. If athletes did not evaluate their opponent's strengths and weaknesses, they might as well just not turn up to the competition at all.

My Experience as an Athlete

When I prepare for a bout, there are always several monitors set up all around the ring. In this way, while I practice I can always have a look at fight videos of my next opponent. I need to internalize his movement patterns, his attacks and his defense intensely in order to be able to use this information during the fight. The more I can prepare myself for this opponent, the better I will be in the ring. This goes as far as almost to become a game of chess: because I have studied my opponent so intensely, I can attune myself to him. Sometimes this works so well that I can predict what he will do next.

My Experience as a Businessman

Like anyone else who has spent their entire working life in one business sector, I know the structures and the players that matter in the world of boxing.

I am aware of their strengths and weaknesses because I learnt them during my time as a boxer, as a promoter, and as an event organizer. I also know what the talents, the professionals, the boxing enthusiasts and the fans want. This led me to realize that the promoting business of old is not working any more. Sporting excellence, the presentation of the athletes, the organization of boxing events... all of these are no longer separate entities but are part of the same these days. We took this on board. Since 2015 the promoter K2, the event organizer KMG, and the marketer for television rights worldwide IMG, have been working together. This furthers our strengths, reduces our weaknesses, and by combining the promoter's, organizer's and marketer's expertise it creates a powerful network for the sportspeople who have signed with us.

Trends in the Business World

"Six is better than six"—Although it looks at first sight like a particularly uninspired slogan, this phrase was an attempt by Samsung to denigrate Apple's then current smartphone. In the commercial, the competing models—Samsung's Galaxy S6 and Apple's iPhone 6—were contrasted with each other. In an attempt to hit a humorous note, the South Korean company points to the supposed strengths of their phone as opposed to the product by their Californian competitor: wireless charging, for example, as well as a wider lens for the front camera. Obviously, Samsung was hoping to gain an advantage by stressing its own strengths and stressing Apple's weak points.

The competition among smartphone producers is getting tougher. For the moment, Apple and Samsung are still the big fish of the business, but the number of competitors is growing. It is therefore hardly surprising that the various parties observe each other's strengths and weaknesses very carefully and at times use them in their communication with the public. What is noticeable is the remarkable speed with which these newcomers are learning from the pioneers of the business. They display no inhibitions at all in their quest eventually to outdo their former role models.

Part III

How Experts Use Challenge Management Practically

I am not the only one to use the solutions described above to tackle and master central challenges. While talking to acquaintances and companions, I noticed that there are parallels between their approaches to solving challenges and my own approach. I have therefore asked twelve well-regarded businesspeople and managers to share with us their answer to one of the central challenges respectively. How, for instance, does an entrepreneur previously spoilt by success deal with having crashed a promising start-up? How does one manage to gain new potential from this defeat? Another contributor is one of the most successful advertising creatives of our time. How has he managed to trust in his own competences and thus to develop top-quality advertising campaigns for decades?

Their answers demonstrate that even in the most diverse sectors and areas the challenges that arise are similar. Be inspired by the solutions these experts are sharing with us.

Coopetition

Frank Dopheide, Managing Director of Handelsblatt publishing group

- Founder of the agency "Deutsche Markenarbeit", previously chairman of the advertising company Grey Worldwide
- Education: Sport University Cologne, special focus on journalism

"Challenges are energizing events that sharpen all of your senses and gather all of your energies in order to surpass yourself and rise above your everyday life."

Milestones

Sport University Cologne: I took my time studying and gained my diploma as a teacher of physical education after 7 years at university. Then suddenly there were far too many trained teachers and not enough jobs to go round for everyone who had finished their university course. Instead of racing ahead professionally, suddenly I was told to go right back to square 1. Luckily, my course had offered a special focus on journalism, and to my surprise I had discovered I was good at writing.

Spiess, Ermisch, Abels: I found the answer in the shape of this advertising agency. One of its founders, Ewald Spiess, saw in me something that I myself was not even aware of. He recognized my creative potential and hired me as a copywriter. He really had a good nose for potential.

I learned, developed, and climbed the career ladder. A few years later I became the creative director at a different agency.

Grey Worldwide: The job as chairman of the agency Grey turned everything on its head. I was the first creative ever to be given this position. It was a fundamentally different job than any other that I had ever done. I needed almost none of the skills that had gained me the position in the first place. Instead of creative sparkle, it was conversations with English controllers, administrative tasks, and management matters that dominated my everyday working life. It became my most important task to recognize the potential of the staff members and to give them the space and energy to fulfill their potential. I was good at this: During that time Grey rose up the rankings to become one of the ten most creative agencies. We won the first Lion in the agency's history at the Creative Festival in Cannes. Business started to boom.

> Coopetition is the combination of cooperation and competition. The idea behind coopetition is that not just cooperative partners but also competitors work together and profit from this collaboration. The driver might be the desire to save resources and to be environmentally friendly. The motivation may also be the desire to share know-how and experiences in order to strengthen one's own position. Even dominant players lack the capacities or competences to implement trends and innovations as quickly as possible all by themselves.

Wladimir Klitschko is convinced:
If you share know-how and experiences even with your competitors, you can strengthen your own position.

"The World Has Become Too Complex to Be Able to Succeed by Oneself"

Project: A subsidiary for digital marketing that is shared with competitors

Competitor/Opponent: Quality media, media houses, internet companies

Challenge: To successfully manage to cross over into digital media, despite being a quality publication rooted in the print business, and to prosper as a small player against large websites with a broad reach.

The rules of the game have changed massively: The situation used to be that there were two dozen national daily or weekly papers. There was a certain target group who considered it a mark of being well bred to read one or two of these quality papers. Each paper had a focus and a political allegiance, and advertisers knew who to reach in what way. But then the internet came along. Media houses and other content originators started providing news and other content online free of charge. Readers switched from print to online media, and the sales figures of printed papers dropped. Advertisers discovered Facebook, Google and YouTube as channels for their commercials.

It took newspaper publishers a while to realize that this was an irreversible trend. And that they needed to act or else they would inexorably lose business to new competitors. The Düsseldorf-based *Handelsblatt* had established an advert marketing channel for digital products early on. However, the company soon found out that compared to the large websites they were small fry. Accordingly, they chose a course of action that would have been unimaginable a few decades earlier: They turned to their competitor papers *Frankfurter Allgemeine Zeitung, Süddeutsche Zeitung* and *Die Zeit* and suggested that together they start a shared digital marketing platform. Their competitors agreed. In truth, they did not have much to lose from it. *Handelsblatt* was more advanced than them technically and in terms of know-how. Furthermore *Handelsblatt* invited them to become partners in its subsidiary IQ Digital.

It has been eight years since the start of this success story. Frank Dopheide at the time had not yet started at the company, but as the current managing director of the *Handelsblatt* group he considers the decision to work together as absolutely right in retrospect: "Coopetition has become a principal survival strategy," he is convinced. "It is no longer the case that the strongest are best off by themselves." The world has grown so complex that companies are no longer able to recognize, pick up and solve upcoming trends and problems. They have not got the necessary budget, the staffing resources or the required competences. Digitalization has sped up this process enormously and has forced industries to totally reinvent themselves—for example the newspaper industry.

"Companies need to recognize that the past no longer defines the present," Dopheide says. Yesterday's guidelines no longer hold, which is why managers would be well-advised not to stick to their old views of who their friends or enemies are. While the competitors of *Handelsblatt* used to be mainly the *FAZ* (*Frankfurter Allgemeine Zeitung*) or *Financial Times Deutschland,* these days the pool is considerably larger, according to Dopheide: National as well as international news providers compete for advertising revenues and users, as do business platforms like Xing or LinkedIn, as well as (online) universities and bloggers.

The most demanding step one needs to take before coopetition can take place is to change the corporate culture. In some companies, as Dopheide has observed, this change process is akin to "pain treatment". What many struggle with is that walls need to be torn down: walls between teams and departments, between companies and even walls to former competitors. To make this work there can only be one driver: The pressure to change has to become larger than their own ego among the decision makers, the brand expert Dopheide thinks. The vision of an outstanding result needs to outshine the fear of failure.

To get the staff to buy in and to reduce resistance in their ranks, his advice to companies is: "Conquer the indifference." This will require acting and thinking in an unfamiliar manner; a visible and tangible change that shakes up the employees' everyday routine. This will make them pay attention to the management's plans and ideas and develop their readiness to follow them.

This kind of change is what Dopheide and his team wanted to achieve in the automotive sector. It is one of the industries that are under pressure. After decades of success, car producers found out to their cost that young people prefer to hire cars than to buy them. They also realized that new competitors have started to challenge them, whether by developing electric vehicles or self-driving cars. "You are letting them run rings around you in terms of communication," Dopheide tells the PR bosses of the big companies. "Tesla and Google are not selling cars, but they are dominating the news reports and are making their mark as the trailblazers."

The idea therefore was for all German car producers to join forces. The German equivalent to Silicon Valley is its automotive industry. They brought together what needed to be together to be ready for the future, as Dopheide phrases it. With BMW, Daimler and Volkswagen he set up an automotive summit. The special thing about this was that this event did not take place in any odd convention center but at BMW World in Munich with Daimler and VW displaying their models right beside those of their competitors. Some members of their staff may have been stunned, but that was just what this coopetition was aiming at: to create a special moment that would take away the breath of everyone present and that would set off an incredible avalanche of energy.

Besides the CEO of BMW Harald Krüger, the chairman of Daimler Dieter Zetsche, and the CEO of VW went on stage within the hallowed halls of BMW to address the staff of all three car companies. They wanted to show their employees as well as the business world at large: Together we need not fear these new competitors from the USA. We are the backbone of the German economy—we have the strength and the power.

In Frank Dopheide's view coopetition will be the most significant economic principle over the next few years. To make coopetition work, however, it will be essential to think big and surprise one's target groups. As Oscar Wilde said: "An idea that is not dangerous is unworthy of being called an idea at all."

Enabling and Using Coopetition

Prerequisites for a Successful Cooperation with the Competition

1. **Security:** Essential for coopetition to work: Do the partners fit each other? Do they share the same values? Does the foundation of product and business model work?

2. **Uncertainty:** If you are already 100 percent sure what the result will look like before you have even started, then this is not the right coopetition. A promising project requires imagination and openness in order to inspire everyone involved.

3. **Perception:** All partners ought to benefit from the coopetition. Then everyone will have their own role and task, a say in terms of the content, and the possibility of making themselves seen.

4. **Belonging:** Coopetition is about working together as partners. This requires active support and visible symbols of the union.

5. **Growth:** The goal of a coopetition is to aid the personal development of the staff, the project and the company.

6. **Being a Part of Something Big Together:** A change in the corporate culture is essential for everyone involved if the coopetition is to succeed. They need to feel that they are a part of something big.

Progressivity

Alyssa Jade McDonald-Bärtl, Founder of Blyss, CACAO Academy and ChangeMaker.Land; previously Head of Department for International Communications, Deutsche Telekom, as well as for Brand and Communication, T-Systems

* Education: Queensland University of Technology in Australia, B.A. in Business Studies and Journalism, Diploma in fitness

"Challenges are situations in which it does not suffice to use my tried and tested methods in order to solve them. A challenge is a moment when I create something new to reach my goal. It's a great chance for learning and developing new ways."

Milestones

Olympic Organizing Committee: Before I started doing Business Studies, I had already studied journalism in Australia. While I was still going to my lectures, I got a job on the team organizing the Olympic Summer Games in Sydney in 2000. I started there as a media officer and learnt incredible amounts. The mood was fantastic and the work international. I enjoyed that time so much that a year later I got involved again, in the preparations for the Olympic Winter Games in Salt Lake City in the USA.

Unternehmensgrün: As a "social entrepreneur" I am very interested in improving the conditions required for a green and ethical economy. I am therefore very involved in the German Federal Association of Green Business, Unternehmensgrün, and represent the interests of its members to political representatives in both Berlin and Brussels. I am frequently invited to give lectures on topics like the circular economy and ethical trade.

Blyss: I have been an entrepreneur full time since 2009. Two years previously I had taken part in the "Ironman" competition in Hawaii, and afterwards I started searching for a new challenge. My father had accompanied me and after the competition was over we tried some raw cocoa at the edge of a cocoa plantation. That proved to be the starting point: It got us thinking about how we could produce chocolate that was good for both body and world in that it was healthy as well as treating the farmers fairly.

Although the theory might sound simple, it is often difficult to put into practice. If you want to create something new, you need to break free from convention, throw out your previous assumptions and change your perspective, and you must not allow yourself to be held back by doubters.

Wladimir Klitschko is convinced:
To think progressively and act courageously means leaving the beaten paths behind and creating your very own solutions. This may well cause us to be afraid, but that isn't a bad thing. To me, being afraid signifies movement and not being cowardly. Whoever finds the courage to be brave for the first time will ask themselves afterwards why they did not dare do that earlier. Every experience makes us grow and mature.

"People Who Tell Me Why Something Won't Work Are Just Looking for Excuses"

Business Idea: To transfer the experience the chocolate producer Blyss gained in sustainable agriculture to ChangeMaker.Land. This consultancy "translates" that knowledge for other industries, adapts and implements it.

Competitor/Opponent: Conventional farmers, food manufacturing and processing companies, consultancies both with and without a focus on sustainability

Challenge: To convince firms that do not think in terms of sustainability of the idea and benefits behind the concept of ChangeMaker.Land and to demonstrate to them that ethics and profits can go hand in hand

Her father's death changed her life. His suggestions had been the starting point for Alyssa Jade McDonald-Bärtl developing a chocolate start-up company that focused on providing the highest-possible quality as well as fair conditions for farmers and producers. For two years the Australian McDonald-Bärtl had been working at setting this up with her father's support. He was on location with the cocoa farmers in Ecuador while she was fine-tuning her ideas in parallel to working full-time at her job in Germany. When she got the phone call telling her that her father was critically ill in hospital she dropped everything and flew out to South America. He died soon after, and the doctors told Alyssa McDonald-Bärtl that the same fate awaited her if she did not look after her health better and drastically change her lifestyle.

She took this on board and quit her stressful executive position at the company. She made the decision to push ahead full-time with her business idea. "That decision meant that I had lost everything", she says with hindsight. Having already lost her father, she also lost her home base in Germany, her job, and her purpose in life. Yet she felt she owed it to her father to keep pursuing their shared vision. And it paid off to carry on by thinking progressively and acting courageously. "I ended up gaining more from this than I could have imagined at the time."

Alyssa McDonald-Bärtl became the third generation of social entrepreneurs in her family. Her parents and grandparents had managed a rubber plantation and run a sustainable cattle farm in the mountains of Papua New Guinea and Australia. Alyssa for her part selected two cocoa plantations in Ecuador that she was going to expand. The cocoa harvested there was going to be used for her chocolate production.

Her courage was rewarded: Nowadays, connoisseurs call her products "the purest chocolate in the world". She has worked with around 400 farming families, trained them and introduced them to a new payment system. Instead of service providers she made the farmers into partners and offered to pay them a commission on their cocoa sales. Furthermore, she advised the farmers about how they might be able to buy land of their own in order to escape the vicious circle of poverty and exploitation by large producers.

The sales aspect of the business is going well, too: Blyss sells their exquisite cocoa to restaurants and hotels across the world, and their stock is regularly sold out before the new harvest is available. A real success story.

At the time, however, it was not at all clear just how big the adventure was that McDonald-Bärtl, the former marketing manager, let herself in for. "I didn't care," is how she describes this step. "My life got back on track the moment I started following my vision and mustered the courage to set my own standards." She used her own values as her guideline and established more sustainable ways of producing and processing the cocoa than the majority of large producers did. Some have since started following her example. Her approach has the potential to change the whole industry.

She has no patience with people who congratulate her now that she is successful, but who brush off how much risk and effort were involved in her endeavors. "I have been given so many reasons why it was, supposedly, easy for me to follow my goals and why the starting conditions for others are, supposedly, so much harder. That is quite simply an excuse that these people come up to soothe their own ego." Thinking and acting progressively always means you have to leave your comfort zone. In this case, it was done with a view to improving both her own situation and that of others.

In 2014, this approach was the catalyst for another brave decision. At the time, Blyss was employing eight staff members, who worked with about 1,000 people on the plantations. "I asked myself the question: Should we concentrate on growing Blyss further or on convincing as many people as possible of our approach?" Alyssa McDonald-Bärtl decided to do the latter and set up "CACAO.academy" as well as "ChangeMaker. Land".

While the academy provides sustainability training for farmers, producers and retailers, ChangeMaker.Land has established itself as a consultancy that advises companies in other sectors and supports them in implementing standards similar to those at Blyss. Among its clients are energy and financial companies, as well as tourism firms and insurance companies. ChangeMaker.Land has developed a program outlining how any company can act more sustainably and in doing so can kick off changes across its entire industrial sector (confer "How to Become a Sustainable Company in Eight Steps").

The founder, Alyssa McDonald-Bärtl, is more than happy with her decision: Blyss is still enjoying success on the market. At the same time, by means of her new companies, she has managed to expand her activities and increase her influence significantly. It is a nice side-effect, as far as she is concerned, that her move has paid off financially, too, because the new businesses make more profit than the chocolate company. A much more important affirmation for her is that her courage has been rewarded. "I led by example and established a recognized standard using my own values, not something that somebody else imposed on me. To me, there could be no bigger success!"

Thinking Progressively and Acting Courageously

How to Become a Sustainable Company in Eight Steps

1. **Understanding Entrepreneurship:** Growth does not equal increasing sales and profit at any cost. Think about how you could improve standards in your industry. Could you cut out the middleman or improve the conditions the producers are working under? Set up a subsidiary and train others in your industry.

2. **Official Standards:** Question the established conditions and standards of your industry. Find out in detail about terms of trade, sanctions and regulations. Get involved when reforms and amendments are being considered, and find supporters in business associations and networks.

3. **Inclusive Growth:** Think about how you might be able to create jobs for the long-term unemployed. Or for mothers, who do not appear in the unemployment statistics but for whom work would bring a real benefit for their overall situation and those around them.

4. **Funding:** Approach financiers who are open to ethical investments. Do your research into what official funding is available and point out these sources to start-ups, suppliers or farmers at the beginning of the value chain.

5. **Technology:** Support start-ups that can help bring innovation to your sector. Offer them mentoring, ease their access to investments and help them expand into other markets.

6. **Change Processes:** Inform important players in your industry of the change you are trying to bring about. Go on road shows and forge links with companies that do not appear, at first sight, to have much

connection to your business: insurers, financial services providers, or analysts, for example.

7. Drivers: Support promising hopefuls and talents from within your industry who are as interested in change as you are. Instead of working with renowned researchers or consultants from your corporate culture, use experts from the country of production. Consult the farmers or producers of your products, who may well have been working in that industry for generations.

8. Sensitivity: Take on the leading role in your industry, and go about your task exuding trust, respect and support. Do not make derogatory remarks about those exponents of your industry who hold different values than you. Always try to achieve the best possible results, and do not insist on conditions that pose too much of a challenge for the majority of your competitors.

Way 3
Defeats

Rolf Schumann, Global GM Platform & Innovation, previously co-founder of the clean-tech venture Better Place; author of the books *Simplify your IT* and *Update. Warum die Datenrevolution uns alle betrifft* (Why the Data Revolution Matters to Everyone)

- Education: University of Mannheim, Germany, Business Informatics; ZfU International Business School Thalwil/Switzerland, IT management

"Challenges are tasks I tackle that I have not encountered before."

Milestones

Siemens Business Services: While I was still studying, I was already working there as a senior consultant. Back then my employer was the largest "technological playground" imaginable. I gained an understanding of the way organizations and people function and, at the same time, how important a good education and sound knowledge are. Most important was maybe that I met the man who has been my adviser, friend, and mentor ever since.

Better Place: This was an enormous experience: I learnt to think and act beyond boundaries and conceptions. I understood why things work and how people act. Unfortunately this resulted in the most devastating professional and social failure of my life. Our idea did not work out, and I learnt the hard way what it means to pick yourself back up when you have hit rock bottom. That was a situation that made me realize who my real friends and family were and who were mere acquaintances or companions.

SAP: As the person in charge of technology for the EMEA region (Europe, Middle East, Africa) it was my responsibility to create and drive innovation. I had to make the best out of the contradiction between size and agility and was able, luckily, to use my experience of being defeated and of the boundaries of technology. By happy coincidence, working at SAP was like finding another family in addition to my actual family.

> We often feel like losers if we have failed at something—whether this be while competing for a contract, competing over a potential employee, or negotiating a pay rise. However, this way of looking at things actually is not beneficial as it does not help us do better and be more successful next time.

Wladimir Klitschko is convinced:
If you are not successful you need to analyze your defeat carefully. The results will help you prepare as best possible for the next challenge. Do not wallow in self-pity. Position yourself as an active doer and shaper of things to come.

"If You Want to Be Successful, You Have to Change People's Behavior"

Business Idea: Clean-tech venture Better Place, which offered electric cars with exchangeable batteries.

Competitors/Opponents: Traditional car manufacturers, filling stations.

Challenge: To change car users' attitudes towards mobility and car usage. After this failed: to learn the necessary lessons from the company's bankruptcy.

He wanted to save the environment and make the world a slightly better place: When Rolf Schumann founded the start-up Better Place in 2008 to produce electric cars with exchangeable batteries, he was one of the trailblazers of the clean car market. Together with the founder Shai Agassi, he won over Renault-Nissan as a partner for a cooperation and built a comprehensive infrastructure for their project in Denmark and Israel. In 2012 they started selling the cars. German car manufacturers like BMW, Daimler, or VW were at that time only just beginning to run their first practical tests with their electric models.

The idea of Better Place was this: It offered its customers a subscription for the electricity needed for the cars. A flat rate of 200 euros per month would thus enable them to drive up to 12,500 miles per year. Included in the price were electricity from renewable sources, maintenance, the use of charging and battery changing stations, as well as a mobility guarantee. Better Place chose Denmark and Israel as its markets because their size was manageable. It had not, however, managed to establish itself in Germany by the time it filed for bankruptcy.

The company had received 950 million US dollars in funds and assets from its financiers. The founders had been feted for their vision and ambition, but in the end the company managed to sell only few of the 100,000 vehicles it had agreed with Renault. "You could say that our idea failed because it was just ahead of its time," Rolf Schumann says. "But really that would just be making excuses", he admits self-critically.

The vision that he and his companions were trying to make a reality was that they would change car drivers' habits. "I am convinced: If I want to be successful, then I need to change people's behavior," Schumann says. Apple's founder Steve Jobs, for example, changed the way we communicate and use smartphones, and Facebook's CEO Mark Zuckerberg created a network that enables people to stay in touch with their friends and acquaintances in a totally new way. In a similar manner, SAP developed a standard for companies to file their invoices and standardize other organizational processes.

Better Place's approach was to try to free car-driving nations from their dependence on oil. In retrospect Schumann realized: Visions such as this only succeed when the customers can see a real benefit for themselves. To appeal to reason alone will not work. Schumann has drawn the following conclusion from his defeat with Better Place: "It is not enough to create a fabulous innovation and to make a perfect product. What customers want is more convenience. And this they don't want for the same price but cheaper."

To begin with, the start-up had conducted a number of marketing studies to find out: Will the product we are offering be interesting to customers? Would they buy it? The feedback was positive. In the end, however, people behaved differently. "They were worried about range," Schumann says. Drivers were concerned they would run out en route because the car batteries had a range of 75 miles, which was smaller than the range that a tank full of gas would provide.

Another significant conclusion that Schumann reached following the failure was: A business will not work if it has been planned and laid out for years ahead. While he says it is good to have a vision, the actors should still be able to change at short notice the plans that were based on this vision. "It is necessary these days for projects to be questioned again and again. Conditions change so quickly and so frequently. Therefore, we need to evaluate challenges and goals all the time and react to changes", the entrepreneur Schumann thinks.

After Better Place ended, Schumann took some time out and then started working at the software company SAP SE again. Previously he had been its representative in charge of technology for the EMEA region, and today he is the Global General Manager for the areas Platform and Innovation. He finds the lessons he learned from the failure of Better Place help him in his new job: "At SAP there are fewer and fewer of the traditional big-bang projects, and instead we run a lot more work packages that are agile, manageable, and generate value immediately." While it used to be normal to plan software rollouts far in advance and to launch mammoth projects that would often span years, the duration of a project nowadays is between six and eight weeks. Several of these will then be run in a chain.

As an example Schumann brings up a template—a kind of digital form for internal processes—that was to be introduced at SAP worldwide.

When it finally arrived at the last branch far from central office, it had long since stopped being relevant. These days there are no more big or protracted projects at SAP, he says. Instead, agile teams develop lean concepts and start rolling them out in close consultation with the respective clients. These clients can be customers or industry players.

This idea was also a result of Schumann's defeat: So as not to work at cross purposes with what the target group actually wants, a product, project or business idea should be developed from within the circle of those involved in it. That way they can reduce or ideally eliminate the danger of daring ideas being developed on the drawing board and far from reality instead of being closely aligned with the wishes and needs of clients throughout the planning process. For this, Schumann, like SAP as a whole, uses "Design Thinking" workshops, whose aim it is to solve the clients' problems by looking at them together with the user and from the perspective of the user to develop new ideas.

Had he done that at Better Place all those years before, he might have found out what drivers really wanted from a battery that was going to succeed in changing their attitude towards mobility. A possible result might have that they wanted a range of at least 250 miles. Another might have been that they wished for more charging stations. Whether these desires could have been fulfilled by means of an innovation is another question entirely, but at least it might have called into question the business idea of Better Place.

In principle it is a simple matter, Rolf Schumann thinks: If the focus is on the customer then many aspects will fall into place by themselves. Because then only services and products are being developed that are actually needed by a target group. It is also important not just to develop that idea once and then to let it run its course. "We have to ask ourselves all the time: Is customer behavior changing? And if so, are we able to adjust what we offer?"

As a manager, when Schumann listens to colleagues and notices that their discussion is going round in circles, he likes to tell them the following joke. It clarifies what the priorities are in a simple way:

A dozen managers at a dog food company are sat in a conference room together. One of them is giving a presentation and projecting sales curves, target group segments and pie charts. The reason for the meeting: Their new product has been selling worse than expected, and they are trying to find the reason. They analyze the sales channels, discuss the cost structure, look at the social media activities, and even think of expanding the advertising campaign to the television. A member of the catering team, who has come in to check the drinks supply, joins the conversation: "I'm sorry to interrupt, but have you thought about whether dogs actually like the food?"

Learning from Defeats to Create New Potential

A Method for Systematically Working through Defeats

1. **Analyze the Defeat:** Allow a few weeks to go by, and then analyze what happened and be brutally honest: What went wrong and where? What mistakes could have been avoided? What mistakes did you yourself make?

2. **Draw Potential from the Defeat:** Once you know what was good about your business idea and what the crucial error was: exchange your insights with other founders and businesspeople, learn from each other and perhaps develop a new idea that promises to be more successful.

3. **Put Customer Focus at the Center:** Before you throw yourself into the next adventure: do not develop any project with a circle of colleagues or other like-minded people. Instead, speak to potential customers and find out what problem you are trying to solve with your product or service. Design Thinking workshops are the perfect setting for such conversations.

4. **Be a Game Changer!:** Try to use your product offer to effect a change in behavior—for the better—among customers. Only then has your offer got the makings of becoming truly successful.

5. **No More Five-year Plans:** Do not set your plans in stone, not even for the next three years. Work in such a way that you can react at short notice to customer wishes or changed market conditions.

Successes

Ibrahim Evsan, founder of Connected Leadership, serial founder (3rd Place, United Prototype, Fliplife, sevenload, Social Trademark)

• Education: Advertising manager, followed by independent study

"Challenges motivate me afresh every day. Really what they mean is solution-oriented working."

Milestones

Coming of Age: I come from an immigrant family. I left home aged 17, having finished school after 10th grade with a low pass. I am glad that despite my poor grades I had the courage to move away from my family and take my life into my own hands. I had reached the conclusion that deep-rooted conflicts cannot be resolved through talking.

Adulthood: It has been a long way, but it has been worth it. The years and decades after moving out I spent getting to know myself. I allowed myself to recognize my weaknesses and mistakes and to accept them. In parallel, I was working at my professional career. Basically, anything I know and am able to do, I have taught myself. My self-reliance taught me always to be forward-looking in my thinking.

Maturing: These days I regularly work at controlling my thoughts. By this I mean always thinking positively and not to get the blues if things are not going well. It also means placing the issue or other people, rather than my own ego, at the forefront of my thoughts. I have to admit: This is a task that is, and probably always will remain, work in progress.

> Those who are successful should give back to society so that society can grow. This idea is one of the basic principles of a social market economy.

Wladimir Klitschko is convinced:
If you share, you do not just help others but also benefit yourself. The feedback makes the teacher a learner; the giver himself, as it were, becomes the receiver of a gift. Furthermore, I consider it a matter of course to give back to those who are younger or less privileged and to let them share in my success.

"Knowledge that Gets Saved but not Shared, Is Wasted"

Project/Business Idea: Building up knowledge, sharing knowledge

Competitors/Opponents: Agencies, advisers, bloggers, speakers, media experts

Challenge: Keeping knowledge constantly and comprehensively up-to-date

Ibrahim Evsan talks the talk and walks the walk: He is a digitalization expert who has founded and built up five companies over the last twelve years. All of them are to do with the internet—from a platform for the free-of-charge management of multimedia content (sevenload) to an agency that professionalizes the online presence of specialists in order for them to present themselves in the best possible way online (Social Trademark). All of these companies reflect his own development: "Knowledge that gets stored but not lived or shared, is wasted," he says. He has the drive to build new knowledge constantly, to use it and to eventually pass it on. This also means using his own successes and sharing them with others. "It also requires me to be open, and sometimes brave enough and ready, to optimize myself."

Ibrahim Evsan is a veteran of digital and social media. For 20 years now he has been active in the digital sector, and for the last ten years as a blogger and social media expert. Whenever the occasion presents itself, he speaks at big events about his experiences.

For him, the rise of the internet was a real blessing, he says. Previously, he regularly met up with four or five friends to exchange views about topics he was interested in or that were part of his specialism: How is society changing? What influence do technological innovations exert? What impact does internationalization have on the population? These exchanges he found inspiring, yet he also noticed the limitations of the range of opinions present and of the impact of the exchanges. Since the internet gained traction, he has therefore moved these exchanges of opinion to the online sphere. He publishes his ideas in his blog or on social media, which brings him in contact with countless experts. "This multitude of potential contacts meant that my reach suddenly grew much bigger, as well as giving me access to an incredible plurality of opinion and expertise. The exchanges were great fun because we stimulated each other."

All of this used to be essentially a hobby but has long since grown into a business. He has 100,000 people following him online. He now also publishes about the experiences he has drawn from his undertakings and passes on knowledge that will be helpful to others. He himself profits from this, too, as he has become one of the most sought-after keynote speakers for conferences and symposia dealing with digital topics. He thinks that he only gets booked for these events because he addresses topics that serve the public good. Even business ideas have sprung from his experiences, such as his most recently founded enterprise, in early 2017, called "Connected Leadership". This is an agency providing advice about all aspects of the digital transformation. This agency was possible only because he had always been ready to give advice, both theoretical and practical, in conversations beforehand and constantly built up his expertise.

Ibrahim Evsan's example demonstrates in a very impressive way that sharing knowledge free of charge is not a one-way street. If his know-how has a high value-added factor, then many people will be prepared to pay for it by, for example, booking him as a speaker or by paying a fee to use his services.

In order to ensure that the mutual stimulation of his activities continues to work, he spends a lot of effort on his online reputation, namely his social media presence, his blog and his website. At least twelve working hours each week are spent on maintaining his online reputation. Serial founder Evsan recommends that experts spend ten percent of their income on online advertising in order to keep their business going and growing.

Evsan also expects that top managers, too, should have more online presence. "The connected society is continuously growing in importance," he says. "Customers and employees expect companies to be connected and to have a connected CEO at the top." However, Evsan adds that although CEOs need not be as intensely engaged online as he himself is, they have to be open to the issue of online presence.

His advice to top managers is not to put this issue off. "Those who get started first will end up the winners. After all, there are only ten positions on the first page of Google's search result rankings."

Making Use of Your Successes and Letting Others Partake in Them

Five Steps Towards Building a Professional Online Reputation

1. **Technology:** It is not enough for a website or a blog to look good. It is at least as important that the content you put on it is optimized for Google and the relevant systems, that it enables maximum interaction, and that service providers can intuitively handle the system.

2. **Positioning:** How are you going to position yourself and what aspect of expertise do you want to accentuate? These questions need to be considered thoroughly because anything you publish from then on ought to be based on this positioning.

3. **Contents:** Do not let yourself be tempted to publish as much as possible in an effort to demonstrate your expertise. Instead, whet your target group's appetite with a few choice contributions and then offer products or services as an extension. If you write a blog, then choose not the latest hot topics but issues that will remain topical for weeks and even months. Be careful to give a positive impression; talk about your successes. No-one will follow you if all ever you do is moan.

4. **Images:** Have professional (portrait) photos taken. Choose a photographer who is known and active on social media as this will have a positive effect on your online hits and rankings.

5. **Social Media:** Make use of all social media channels that could be useful for your business. Get to know the specifics of each platform and align your contents accordingly. Never spread the same message in the same wording over all channels. Keep an eye on communications and react to questions. If someone has a go at your posts, putting them down, do not enter into a discussion. Follow other authorities on the subject and start a conversation with them.

6. Search Engine Optimization: Invest part of your budget in SEO (Search Engine Optimization) and SEM (Search Engine Marketing). Your texts have to include keywords and other elements that make them easier to find and more valuable for Google.

Planning and Performance

Christian Seifert, CEO of DFL (Deutsche Fußball Liga, the German Football League), previously CEO of Karstadt-Quelle New Media

- Education: University of Essen (Germany)—communication studies, marketing and sociology

"To me a challenge is just that: a challenge! If we want to grow inside, then we can only do that by going to our limits. To keep seeking out these limits; to work up the energy to push the limits in a way that makes sense to me as a person and to us as a company: that seems to me a fitting description of what a challenge is."

Milestones

MTV Network: As director of marketing in Central Europe I held responsibility for B2C and B2B marketing as well as for new media between 1998 and 2000.

Karstadt-Quelle New Media: From 2000 until 2005 I was a member of the board at this company, and from 2004 its CEO. During this time we acquired the TV channel DSF (now called Sport1) as well as the merchandising rights for the 2006 FIFA World Cup in Germany. Our activities at that time were focused on establishing and developing E-commerce and TV commerce.

DFL Deutsche Fußball Liga: In addition to serving as CEO of the DFL, I am a member of the board at the DFL and the vice president of the DFB, the German Football Association (Deutscher Fußball Bund). I recently renewed my contract as CEO until 2022.

If you asked me to pick the most important stage so far, I would not be able to. I don't think that any of the stages on a CV are more or less important than the others. For me, all the stages I went through were important. I could get something from every single one because you can learn from every success and every failure. What mattered more were the people I met and experiences I made. I was lucky to find mentors at many stages of my professional career. Because it does not matter how hard you work: You have to be given the chance to prove what you can do. Success, an older colleague once told me, always has three components: being given a chance, recognizing a chance, and making use of a chance.

> If you want success, you need visions and goals—coupled with stamina

Wladimir Klitschko is convinced:
Some results can come about by chance. Big endeavors, however, can only be implemented if they are based on a vision with a long-term strategy, which we can work towards continuously.

"What Matters Is the Result"

Project: Awarding media rights for the German Football League

Competitors/Opponents: Foreign professional football (soccer) leagues, all media with a wide reach that are trying to address and find viewers or users

Challenge: Marketing and selling the football rights for four years within a short tendering period; increasing profits by opening up new markets and business areas

Time after time the German Football League (Deutsche Fußball Liga, DFL) announces a new record concerning the sale of the Bundesliga media rights. The last record was ca. 4.6 billion euros for a duration of four years, which translates into ca. 1.15 billion euros for the media rights each season. This success speaks for itself, and Christian Seifert's contract as CEO of DFL has recently been renewed until 2022. He has been in charge of the DFL's business operations since 2005. Under his leadership, over the past ten years the marketing of the Bundesliga has grown ten times more quickly than the German economy as a whole.

Of course, as he readily concedes, he cannot take all the credit for this. There are 250 employees in the group of companies, of whom 80 work for the parent company. The core team dealing with the bids consists of five staff. They spend years working towards the goal of being able to address the media at the end of that period and announce the new result.

This mode of operation at the DFL is a prime example of what it means to think in the long term and to continuously demonstrate performance. "'Ongoing Business' with a neuralgic decision-making moment" is what the CEO calls this method that he and his team use. This is because at the end of the four years there is a short period of just a few weeks during which the bidding process is on and all arrangements with TV, internet and mobile phone providers have to be negotiated and contractually agreed.

"Errors during that critical phase can be repaired only to a very limited extent", the DFL CEO stresses. "At those crucial moments we have to get it right. Obviously we prepare as well as we can, but gut feeling is always needed, too."

In the German Football League there were never any mistakes during the critical phase that had a discernible impact. Handball fans, however, experienced in early 2017 that the sale of media rights ahead of major sporting events is far from being an easy process leading to sure-fire success. None of the German TV channels succeeded in securing the broadcasting rights for the men's handball world championship in France. This was because of the complicated contracts the between the owners of the media rights and the International Handball Federation and. Only the last-minute involvement of one of the advertising partners of the German Handball Federation made the games available to watch as an internet live stream.

For German handball this was a missed opportunity. For the Football League, on the other hand, it would have been a catastrophe: without TV broadcasts it has no reach, without reach no sponsors, without sponsors no income. The individual clubs are highly dependent on the income they get from the sale of the media rights. The percentage varies depending on the club but, according to Christian Seifert, makes up between 10 and 50 percent of their total income. Accordingly, the DFL approaches the task very professionally. Soon after the rights have been sold, the team starts working on preparing the next cycle of the bidding process for four years later.

There are four aspects that the DFL prepares with military precision:

- **Legal Framework:** Because the DFL dominates the market in terms of marketing the German Football League, the antitrust authority keeps a very close eye on the bidding process for the rights. For example, it ensures that the matches are not only shown on pay-TV but also on free-to-view channels. Seifert states that in addition to a clear concept, it is essential also to have transparency in communication to ensure that the process goes smoothly.

- **Technology:** Four years is a very long time in the development of TV and telecommunications technology. As a matter of fact, the DFL even has to try to anticipate what the markets are going to look like in eight years' time to ensure that their broadcasting rights are still going to be attractive towards the end of the life of the contract. Today, television, internet, and mobile phone rights are an obvious necessity, but who would have predicted ten years ago that people would watch television on their smartphones? Digital piracy is another topic that the experts at DFL deal with in depth so as to continue to curb abuses of the media rights.

- **Viewers:** How will soccer fans consume football league matches in four, six, or eight years' time? Will they prefer summaries on TV or short clips on their iPhones? Or live broadcasts on YouTube? What impact do decisions regarding the media rights have on physical match-day attendance in the stadium? To find the answers, the DFL conducts extensive market research. The results of the research get compared and balanced with its own experience of many years, and suitable formats are developed on that basis.

- **Media Companies:** The ideas of the various different channels also need to be aligned with each other. Free-to-view channels need to be harmonized with pay-TV companies as well as with mobile phone services and internet providers worldwide. In 2008, in order to stabilize the then still weak pay-TV scene in Germany, the DFL introduced a game at 6:30 p.m., which is broadcast exclusively on Sky. This drew the wrath of those in charge at ARD, a public service broadcaster, which had always shown its own highlights program for that day's matches at just that time. However, the pay-TV channel managed to gain new customers wanting to see the live match, without the ARD losing viewers. Before the DFL took this step, they had conducted extensive customer research that led them to expect this outcome.

Like any other business, the DFL aims to grow. Yet this is not as easy as it sounds if the main source of its revenue is the German broadcasting rights for the matches. After all, the DFL cannot just drive up the price of the rights endlessly. New formats such as the arrangement with Sky are therefore a way of increasing the revenue. This principle applies even more with regard to worldwide marketing. This is where Seifert sees the biggest opportunities for future growth. The German Football League is one of the six largest professional leagues in the world and has fans in all countries of the world. This is reflected in the DFL's sales figures: Ten years ago, Seifert says, the share of sales of marketing rights abroad made up less than 5 percent of all media rights sales. This has now grown to about 20 percent.

Also, wherever the fans are watching the matches, they should do it enthusiastically. The CEO of DFL sees enabling the fans to be enthusiastic supporters as part of his remit. The games have to be attractive. The sport has to be "clean", which means without betting scandals or match fixing by manipulating the results. The sporting level also has to be comparable with other world-class leagues, such as the English Premier League or the Spanish La Liga. This requires constant reflection and communication with clubs, media companies, fans, institutions, and other leagues. Because it matters to think long-term and continuously demonstrate performance.

Officially, Seifert's job is CEO of the DFL, but really he is a diplomat.

Over the course of four years he has to promote soccer and engage in detail with the opinions and ideas of all interested parties and stakeholders to ensure that the Bundesliga maintains its outstanding position. Only by maintaining the mutual exchange with them can Seifert find out what innovations they have tried and what the DFL can learn from them.

All of this he does to serve one single goal: for the Bundesliga to remain one of the strongest sporting leagues in the world. This aim requires finances, which is why economic success in marketing the media rights is so important. The next cycle of the bidding process is sure to come, the CEO states, and then the next one after that. It is not Christian Seifert's style to boast in public about his successes. There is just one comment, which was used by the brand "Under Armour" in a commercial featuring Michael Phelps: "It's what you do in the dark that puts you in the light." To put it simply: what matters is the result.

Thinking Long-Term and Continuously Demonstrating Performance

How to Keep Your Eyes on the Prize during a Marathon

1. **Define Your Goal:** What is it that you want to have achieved in one, two, or four years' time? It has to be something big, important, visionary to be worthwhile thinking about it long term, working towards it for such a long time, and not giving up along the way.

2. **Start the Preparations Immediately:** Do not lapse into inactivity just because the goal still seems so far away. Start working immediately but without succumbing to knee-jerk activism.

3. **Think in Scenarios:** Do not make rigid plans. Instead develop scenarios in your mind. What possible ways are there in which you could implement your vision? Decide on one that is practical and change the chosen approach if necessary. Stay agile.

4. **Determine the Sequence:** Despite all that agility, however, do determine what steps have to be taken at the start, what partners have to be involved early on, and what logical steps have to be taken second, third, fourth etc.

5. **Check Your Performance Regularly:** Create routines in order to demonstrate performance all the time. Arrange regular phone calls or meetings with colleagues in which you inform each other about the progress made. Decide on work packages to be completed by the time of the next conversation.

6. **Celebrate Reaching Milestones:** Do not just focus on the remaining work but enjoy what you have already achieved. Keep what has been accomplished in the forefront of you mind, appreciate the work your team does, and buy everyone a drink at the next meeting.

Reflection

Miriam Goos, CEO of Stressfighter Experts, physician; previously neurologist at University Hospital Göttingen, Germany

- Education: University of Hamburg, Germany, degree and doctorate in medicine

"Challenges mean that I move out of my comfort zone at full power."

Milestones

King's College London: I completed a placement in the department for internal medicine with the Queen's personal physician. I was impressed with the level of discretion people displayed in their work there and with the incredible wealth of knowledge as well as the extremely high standards.

University of Hamburg: I wrote an experiment-based scientific research study for my doctorate in biochemistry under the supervision of Professor Ulrike Beisiegel. It taught me a huge amount, much of which was fundamental: How do I set up the experiments? What does each result show me? What can I deduce from the results and what am I therefore going to investigate as a next step? This goes all the way to the big question: How does science actually work?

University Hospital Göttingen: Under the guidance of Professor Gerald Hüther I worked in scientific research in the area of neurobiology. The most formative experiences during that time were the discussions in the laboratory that ranged far beyond just the results: What did they mean for our world, for the teaching and learning? What environment did we require to be able to reach our full potential, whether in schools, in the workplace, or in everyday life? These discussions were truly exciting.

> Successful executives are good at many things: they are assertive, think strategically, are able to motivate others and keep calm in turbulent times. What many of them need some extra help with, though, is relaxation.

Wladimir Klitschko is convinced:
From top athletes you can learn that hard work has to be followed by a period of rest and relaxation. In the long run, tension cannot work without relaxation.

"Stress is Helpful, but Permanent Stress Harms Us"

Business Idea: Effective program for preventing stress aimed at executives and staff

Competitors/Opponents: Coaches, trainers, and consultants

Challenge: Making people change their attitudes and behaviors

There was a key moment that gave Miriam Goos the idea for her business: She was working as a neurologist in the emergency room of the University Hospital Göttingen when a young woman was brought in. She was an ambitious events manager who had collapsed at work totally out of the blue. In the following weeks her condition worsened. She increasingly suffered from headaches and dizziness and also lost feeling in one arm and one cheek. Goos told her patient she thought that her symptoms may be a result of stress or fatigue, but the patient herself strongly rejected this suggestion. The doctors examined her extensively with diagnostic procedures but could find no physical causes of any sort. They came to the joint decision that the only possible cause was psychosomatic. Goos therefore prescribed an antidepressant and recommended physiotherapy. Over the years, the young woman kept returning to the hospital. Although her condition each time was better than when she was first admitted, she had never regained her previous health. With a maximum result of 50 percent she was working at less than half her previous capacity.

Miriam Goos thought often about this young woman who was still so early in her career. She was appalled at how badly this patient had obviously looked after herself. "And I was shocked by how fast and how far people can fall if they do not pay attention to the warning signals their body sends them." She also became increasingly frustrated with her work as a doctor because she felt that medicine acts too late and with too little regard for the actual underlying causes. She decided to give up her hospital job and to set up a company focusing on stress prevention programs.

The numbers are indeed alarming: 40 years ago only 2 percent of all sick leave was due to mental health reasons, while today this has gone up to about 15 percent. The overall number of sick days is now five times as high as it was, and the average duration of mental health sick leave is 36 days, which is triple that of other illnesses.

"Today we switch off naturally far less than we used to", says Goos, the CEO of Stressfighter Experts. The overstimulation and distraction by our numerous means of communication mean that rest periods, during which we actually and totally switch off, are eliminated. Also, many people have a tendency to stress themselves out with their leisure activities. Further stress multipliers can be found in people's own sense of perfectionism, the high expectations they have of themselves, an inability to say no, fear of losing control, and excessive demands that they may face, Goos says.

Fundamentally, stress is a positive thing, Goos emphasizes. She goes on to describe a ski tour she did with Bavarian friends, during which she was perpetually towards the back of the group. That is, until there was the danger of an avalanche: suddenly Miriam Goos released an incredible amount of energy and managed to reach a safe plateau—at exactly the same time as her friends. This demonstrates that stress is helpful. Yet when stress becomes permanent, it causes health problems. If you have not had any rest for more than eight weeks then it becomes difficult ever to reach a relaxed state again.

Using rest periods for reflection therefore is of the utmost importance in keeping our stress levels within healthy parameters. Rest periods give our minds the space to find out: In what respects may I need to relieve strain? They also make us think: What is my driver, what jolts me into action? When do I manage to surpass myself? What is that I am good at doing? And is it this that motivates me?

Just as important as maintaining a healthy mental balance is taking good care of our bodies. Enough exercise, good sleep, balanced nutrition as well as enough rest breaks are the foundation for a healthy body or, as Miriam Goos calls it, the "most important life partner you'll ever have." Yet, rather than coming up with a big master plan for a healthy life that just keeps getting postponed from one week to the next, we should start by making small changes and building them into our everyday lives. She recommends, for example, regularly taking two to three deep breaths while we are waiting at red traffic lights. Build this into your "autopilot" and eventually you will take deep breaths automatically at each set of red lights. Another tip of hers is what is called the Power Position: sitting upright for two minutes. This is not just good for our backs, but also for self-confidence and inner harmony.

If body and mind are relaxed and strong, this aids development into a resilient person. Resilience means mental hardiness. For mastering crises and for using them as a cause for development by making us draw on our own resources. This also includes assessing situations realistically and not immediately succumbing to panic or fear.

Miriam Goos names seven factors that particularly resilient people have in common:

- realistic optimism: approaching projects positively and confidently without considering worst-case scenarios
- goal orientation: focusing on a result rather than just allowing themselves to drift along

- functioning impulse control: consciously steering reactions and controlling inappropriate actions
- confidence in their self-efficacy: becoming active and taking on responsibility; not viewing themselves as victims
- empathy: being able to put themselves in another person's place and imagine their feelings; not devaluing their actions
- emotion control: dealing appropriately with good as well as bad emotions
- reflective ability: being able to make connections between cause and effect

If you are stuck on the hamster wheel you have not got the opportunity to reflect on yourself and your experiences. As a neurologist, Goos knows that people need distance and some peace and quiet to be able to question their behavior and hold a mirror up to themselves. Recent scientific research has shown that reflection does not just lead us to consider ourselves but that it also brings about concrete changes in the structures involved in the thought processes. Neuroplasticity is the name of this phenomenon, which enables us to change our brain structures in a targeted manner. Put simply it means that merely by reflecting we can change synapses, nerve cells or whole brain areas. "We humans are creatures of habit," Miriam Goos explains, "our thought patterns move along highways in the brain. When we reflect, we are opening up new roads." Just by means of this act of imagination people create new facts in the brain. It takes 40 days of regular implementation for the old highways to wither away if people consistently practice a new behavior.

Simple exercises can give the desired result, for example if it is about doing more for your health. One example would be to take the stairs: ignoring the elevator and walking up the stairs to the first-floor office is something that even unathletic people can manage. It is a small effort that causes them very little struggle. Yet there is some struggle involved. They have to keep their intention in their mind every day; motivate themselves towards the direction of the stairs while others are waiting at the elevators; convince themselves of the sense and purpose of their changed behavior. Once they have done that for 40 days, they no longer even have to think about it. The elevator no longer registers as an option because the corresponding highway in the brain has withered away.

Using Rest Periods for Reflection

Solutions for how to deal with stress:

1. **Reflect:** Lean back and observe: What is it that disturbs you and weighs you down?

2. **Pause:** When you recognize a cause of stress, pause immediately. You have to deal with this villain at once.

3. **Change it:** The next time you find yourself in a similar situation, get active at once. Consciously change your behavior and take a route that serves you better. Consciously practice this behavior to make it second nature.

4. **Aide-memoire:** If the cause of stress sneaks in through the backdoor, then make sure you keep it in the spotlight. You could, for example, put an egg timer on your desk to signal to yourself that you will not allow yourself to be stressed by your boss's hectic demands. Whenever you see that egg timer you will automatically grow calmer.

5. **Document it:** Write it all down: When did you manage to recognize the cause of stress at first sight? When did you manage to change your behavior? And when did you not even get annoyed at the provocation anymore? It is helpful to write such a "mental diary" in order to make your wish become a reality. Take a rest from time to time and read your diary.

Essentials

Jens Schmelzle, founder of the instructional video provider simpleshow, co-initiator of the founder center Start-up-Campus Stuttgart

- Education: Stuttgart Media University (Hochschule der Medien), Germany: degree in audiovisual media

"Challenges force me to move out of my comfort zone. That does require effort but usually reaps its rewards."

Milestones

Independent composer and musician: My big dream was to become a rock star. I was in the band "Submarien" with friends, we were touring both in Germany and abroad, and in 2006 we won the Deutscher Rockpreis award for rock music. Being a musician means much more than just being creative. Really, we were entrepreneurs who were setting up a business: songs, concerts, marketing, organization—I learnt so much, it was incredible. When I founded simpleshow these experiences were enormously helpful.

simpleshow: It was chance that led us to found the instructional video company. It started out as three people in a basement and then we built it up into an international company with sales in the tens of millions. If anyone had told me that beforehand, I would have thought they were mad. This success was based on a healthy mixture of brains, heart and, the necessary luck.

3denker, Pioniergeist, Start-up Campus Stuttgart: The founding team of simpleshow also created several other businesses. Among these is the company Pioniergeist with its Activatr program: It brings together established companies and founders and helps them develop new business models and set up start-ups together.

> The world is full of possibilities, and digitalization and globalization seem to provide a wealth of business opportunities. Yet this view can be fatal: If you try to use too many opportunities at once, you run the risk of getting bogged down and not achieving anything in the end.

Wladimir Klitschko is convinced:
It is advisable to concentrate on one significant goal at a time and, in doing so, to focus on your own ability. Full concentration, therefore, on comparatively little—and following this through consistently.

"Executives Who Can Explain Something Difficult in Simple Terms Have an Advantage"

Business Idea: To explain complex content simply in short videos

Challenge: To simplify while getting across the essentials

His first client was a software producer with a sales problem. This company explained the advantages of its product in such a complicated way and with so much technical detail that hardly anyone could understand it, let alone be persuaded they should buy it.

Jens Schmelzle was a musician back then. Mainly in order to earn the money to set up their own record label, he and two university friends set up a media production company. The request by the software producer was not really what they had in mind, but they went to work anyway.

The goal: a short film. In their basement office they had neither a studio nor a camera, yet they were all sure of one thing: they wanted to use images, not complicated terminology and boring texts. With the help of some friends they produced a video telling a little story about the solution that the software was going to provide. It was simply drawn on paper, used simple pictures that were pushed into the shot one after the other, and made do without any subject terminology or technical language. Recorded on the living room table, they managed to convey the concept congenially, in an easily understood way that inspired confidence. Their client was thrilled.

Soon after they had clients number two and three, and word got around about the young media creatives and their idea. The founders decided to say goodbye to their original idea of media production and to specialize in explainer videos. The company simpleshow was born. Its expertise: to solve the problem of how to give clear explanations.

In the beginning the founders approached their task intuitively. They knew from their media studies course that the attention span of audiences is getting shorter. They also saw in their own environment that pictures and moving images are much more suitable than text for imparting knowledge in a short time.

This led them to the realization that they never wanted to work with written texts. Their videos were to be no longer than three minutes, and they would always use simple images that were explained by a narrator.

Today, simpleshow is the largest provider of instructional videos in the world and the founders' rock band has long since been consigned to history. Around 10,000 videos have been produced by the Stuttgart-based company so far. Simpleshow employs more than 150 staff in eleven locations, who work in more than 50 languages. It runs its own academy, which spends several months training the so-called "concepters" in how to make simple explainer videos.

There are five rules that provide the basic ingredients of a good film (see also "Focus on the Essentials—Applying the Method to a Presentation"):

1. Change of perspective: Put yourself in the audience's place. What prior knowledge do they have, what interests them?

2. Simplification: Drop anything that is not essential.

3. Storytelling: Tell a story rather than just listing facts.

4. Visualization: Use images. They will stay with your audience for much longer.

5. Trust: This is the aim of your explanations: the audience builds trust in the topic. They develop the self-confidence to deal with the subject matter because they have understood the basic principles. You therefore empower them both in terms of knowledge and motivation.

These five points provide a good guideline for the simpleshow concepters as to how to develop a video.

One question remains: What do they tell us during the presentation? How do they decide which aspects to leave out and how do they break down complex matters into easily understandable chunks? How do they focus on the essentials?

The most important rule at simpleshow is to start with "why", meaning the explanation of the subject matter, before moving on to "how", namely the description of individual steps. If you do not explain why something is important, why a product is launched, or why a department gets restructured, then nobody is going to be interested in "how", of this Jens Schmelzle is convinced.

What matters for the explanation is that you choose a tangible analogy based on the area of knowledge of the target audience. If, for instance, Schmelzle wanted to explain centrifugal force to a child, he would choose as an example a swing carousel. Children will be familiar with the feeling of being pushed to the outer edge of their seat as the carousel goes round.

If your target audience were adults, then an example drawn from driving a car would probably be better. If you take the corner too quickly, the car gets pushed towards the outer edge and may even go off the road. The centrifugal force is experienced very obviously in that situation: Drivers have to reduce their speed before they enter the bend or else they might skid off the road. Many a car driver will have experienced this at least to a certain extent.

As another example let us look at ice, meaning frozen water. To explain this to children, Schmelzle would show them that a lake is full of water in the summer, but in the winter when the temperature drops below the freezing point of 0 degrees Celsius, it freezes into ice. The same thing happens if they put a container of water into the freezer. It comes out as a solid ice cube, but it turns slowly back into water if they leave it at room temperature.

If you address adults then you would assume that they already have this prior knowledge, and therefore the narrator can start directly with the chemical processes. Water forms crystals when it freezes because below its freezing point the thermal excitation between the molecules is smaller than the mutually attracting force between the positively charged hydrogen atoms and the negatively charged oxygen atoms. This is how a liquid becomes a solid.

The general rule for simplifying messages is as follows: If the presenter is speaking to lay people then he or she ought to focus much more on the "why". If, however, the presentation is for experts and people with subject knowledge, then he can talk much more about the "how".

These rules, as Schmelzle stresses, apply to every kind of explanation:

- A salesperson trying to draw attention to his or her product should enumerate the advantages of it (Why should the customer buy it?) instead of describing its details (What are the technical details of the product?).
- For an HR manager trying to outline changes in the organization to the workforce it will be helpful to first calm employees' fears and foster self-confidence (Why are the measures important for the future success of the company and the workforce?) instead of detailing the process of how the change will proceed.

Executives in particular ought to try to master the art of explaining things simply, Jens Schmelzle says. After all, their job is not to manage knowledge but rather to pass it on and thus empower others to master new challenges. And, he adds, the good thing is: "A simple explanation is not a God-given talent but a craft that one can learn."

Focus on the Essentials

Applying the Method to a Presentation

1. In order to explain simply, you need to change perspective: Put yourself in your audience's shoes. What is their level of knowledge? What interest do they have in your presentation? What is the mood in which you and your audience meet?

2. Shake off "the curse of knowledge": Omit complicated backgrounds and have the courage to leave out details and exceptions. Even if you have so much more to say about the topic: restrict yourself to the basics.

3. Start your presentation by answering the question of "why": A good explanation is always based on causal relations. If the listeners know why something happens, they will understand the topic faster than if you were to describe to them the "how", meaning the characteristics.

4. Everyone can spare three minutes, but no-one 30: Use the attention span of your audience to spark their interest, not to describe your topic in as much detail as possible.

5. Be a storyteller: Tell a little story. Imagine that you were trying to teach a child something. Everyone prefers listening to an entertaining anecdote than to a list of facts. Make use of analogies drawn from the everyday life of your audience.

6. Visualize your story: Think in images and use these to communicate. This will automatically force you to describe simple matters. Also, images are hugely helpful in expressing and addressing emotions.

Way 8
Competences

Jean-Remy von Matt, founder, owner and director of creative agency Jung von Matt, previous career stages included Springer & Jacoby, Eiler & Riemel, Ogilvy & Mather, as well as BMZ

- Education: diploma as advertising manager in Switzerland

"Challenges appear like a mental mountain that I have to get over in order to get any further. This requires courage, perseverance, and the right preparation."

Milestones

BMZ Baums, Mangs, Zimmermann: When I was looking for my first job in 1974 I went about it quite haphazardly. I applied for positions as advertising consultant, media planner, and creative in Düsseldorf, Vienna, and Zurich. That I ended up at BMZ in Düsseldorf was pure chance. I often asked myself later on what my career path might have looked like had I started it differently. Yet at the time I could not afford to be picky. It was during the time of the oil crisis, advertising budgets were at rock bottom, and many agencies had stopped hiring.

Springer & Jacoby: Twelve years later I changed jobs and went to Hamburg as managing partner for Springer & Jacoby. I had had more lucrative job offers, but I was determined to work at what was then the best creative agency. The change could not have been more drastic: I came from a small but select Munich agency. Springer & Jacoby, by comparison, was a dog-eat-dog environment. It was a turbulent and exciting time during which I met Holger Jung.

Jung von Matt: Together we founded our own agency in 1991. My choice of partner turned out to be extraordinarily fortunate as we complemented each other perfectly. Even though I had been active in the advertising business for such a long time by then, founding our own company posed entirely new challenges. I had to move beyond my comfort zone in many regards in order to make this undertaking a success.

> "Horses for courses", an old proverb says. It only partially gets across what it means to trust in your own competences: to know your strengths, to use them and allow them to unfold beyond the same old routine. Employ them to the best effect.

Wladimir Klitschko is convinced:
This attitude creates self-assurance and the certainty of doing the right thing.

"I do not adorn myself with pretend competences"

Topic: To sparkle with creativity all life long. To preserve, further develop, and constantly question competences.

Opponents/competitors: All creatives and would-be creatives. Other attention seekers.

Challenge: To continue to be part of the elite of creatives and to be perceived as such on the market. Not to allow yourself to lose your confidence within your own area of competence.

There are analytic processes for anything and everything. Quite why nobody has ever developed a process to establish where the talents of individual school leavers or university students lie is something that Jean-Remy von Matt finds absolutely incredible. "There is so much talent in the world that is simply not being used," of this he is convinced. Conversely, he also knows a lot of people who would love to reach a particular position but who just don't have what it takes and therefore end up wallowing in self-pity that no-one has recognized their self-diagnosed genius. In von Matt's case it was largely a matter of chance that he ended up becoming a creative in the advertising business. He tried to work out what he wanted his future profession to be in an erratic way, as he calls it. He sought out lots of feedback, searched his own mind, thought through what his strengths and weaknesses were, compared these to his interests, and finally decided that his competences could be applied well within the broad field of advertising. "This was not totally wrong", as he admits today, even though he thinks that he might have been even better if he had become an architect.

It took a while until Jean-Remy von Matt became well known as an advertising creative beyond the circle of his colleagues and clients. There was no sudden breakthrough. Instead it was a long ascent characterized by lots of hard work and countless small steps. Each creative prize got him a bit of renown, a little more recognition. Did they also bring more competence?

Certainly. Having said that, this advertising creative still does not know, even after about 40 years in the business, quite what his competences are. If you ask outsiders however, they are quick to answer. They consider Jean-Remy von Matt a hugely talented copywriter and one of the most creative advertisers in the business. A creative guru is what the media call him. He is the person behind the cheeky, loud motifs in the advertising for Sixt car rentals and also behind the "Geiz ist geil" ("it's cool to be cheap") campaign for the electronics retail chain Saturn.

Is creativity something one can learn? The entrepreneur von Matt thinks that while a certain amount of talent is necessary a lot of practice is also needed. "Talent, discipline, and hard work are the basic building blocks of any career." Sometimes he sees younger colleagues trying so hard to be geniuses, come what may. Needless to say, this does not work.

You need the capacity for abstract thought, the ability to take a step back from the topic and then to approach it from a different angle. Quite simply, you need to loosen up a bit. "It is not a good idea to aim at the optimum", he says. "That's as if a high jumper puts the bar at world record height at the start of training." This is what he advises young colleagues to do: start on the flat and just scribble down uninspired solutions. After that think around the topic and gradually and playfully improve. The largest inhibitor is often that people are afraid of mistakes. But to overcome this fear is something that one can indeed learn.

That sounds understandable enough. Yet how does one trust in there being a great idea, an ingenious solution at the end? Does someone like Jean-Remy von Matt still have any self-doubt whether he can trust in his own competences? Whether he will have a flash of inspiration at the right time? Experience helps him stay relaxed, he says. And he has the ambition to create something convincing, something unique. Yet despite this, even he has no reliable, automatic supply of great ideas.

What he used to find extremely helpful was open and critical discussions with colleagues, the now director says. However, as he grew more important there were ever fewer people around him who were prepared to criticize him. "Although that feels nice, it is harmful." As a result he appreciates the exchanges he has with his grown-up sons even more. "My children and my wife are the only ones who criticize me openly and sometimes laugh at me." Because executives encounter much less external criticism, self-reflection and self-criticism become more important for them, he thinks. In his view, these should be among of the core competences of managers and entrepreneurs, even though he knows that often the exact opposite is the case.

And how about expanding one's competences? Is there still scope left for this after 40 years in the business? "In all jobs that have undergone big changes, ongoing professional development plays an important role," says the 64-year-old. "For us in the advertising business, it is the revolution in the media that forces us to rethink certain things. If you don't keep up with the ball, then the best-case scenario is that you stagnate." For him personally, however, this does not mean that he familiarizes himself in depth with all these developments. He does concern himself with innovation topics, yes, but he does not need to master them all himself, he feels.

His approach to social media demonstrates this: he is fully aware of the significance of social networks. Nonetheless, he does not participate in them actively. On Twitter, he sticks to the role of passive follower, and he has an anonymous Facebook account. "I do not adorn myself with pretend competences", he declares self-confidently.

He still loves challenges, though: at the moment he and his agency are taking on an extension in content. For the first time since the company was founded, Jung von Matt is working on political advertising. First he worked for the Austrian presidential candidate Alexander van der Bellen. After that, German Chancellor Angela Merkel asked him to work for her during her election campaign to secure her fourth term. This is a clear expansion of his competences: election campaign advertising is much more agile than developing, for example, a campaign for a car company, and very different rules and mechanisms apply, as von Matt says. Also, election campaign advertising is much more hectic.

Within the company, the decision to do advertising for the Chancellor was not without its critics, but Jean-Remy von Matt prevailed. His argument was that this election was particularly important because of the political shift towards the Right in other countries. Also, he did not want to let down the Chancellor, who had asked him in person. And at the back of the advertiser's mind may well also have been: this contract has the potential to become the crowning glory to end his career on. Not long after the elections to the Federal Parliament he celebrated his 65th birthday. As an advertiser he really could not pass up this story.

Trust in Your Own Competences

Five Steps for Becoming Aware of Your Own Competence

1. **Definition:** Put into words what competences you have. Be careful: The things you enjoy the most are not always the things you are best at.

2. **Impact:** Ask those around you: What competences do you stand for? How are you being perceived?

3. **Comparison:** Compare wish and reality. Would you prefer to stand for different topics? Then act accordingly going forward.

4. **Growth:** Think about how you could expand your competences. What challenge makes you smarter, what experience benefits your core competences?

5. **Communication:** Make a plan: What articles do you want to write, what presentations do you want to give, in what public discussions do you want to take part in order to sharpen the focus on how your profile is perceived? Cultivate your social media appearances accordingly and practice presenting yourself convincingly. Use every opportunity to make your core competence known.

Potential

Leopold Hoesch, producer, managing director at BROADVIEW TV GmbH (responsible for example for the films *Angela Merkel. Die Unerwartete, Nowitzki. Der perfekte Wurf, Klitschko,* and *Das Wunder von Leipzig*); previously independent producer

• Education: Diploma in Regional Studies, University of Cologne, Germany

"A challenge to me means finding the best story in history and to tell it perfectly."

Milestones

Founding BROADVIEW TV GmbH in 1999: I always dreamt of setting up my own company like my ancestors had. The goal was to combine television and internet and to build social communities around moving image content. However, I learnt the hard way that it is a thousand times worse to have an idea that is ahead of its time than one that is too late. After the digital bubble burst in 2000, we went "back to the roots" and started producing classic television again. When the German broadcaster ZDF gave us the contract for producing *Stalingrad*, we had our breakthrough. For this three-part German-Russian coproduction we took on part of the financial risk, but for this we gained the right to market the film internationally after it had been aired domestically. We sold the film in 140 countries and won an Emmy for it. Today we are the leading independent producer of movie documentaries in Germany.

Cinedom Cologne: 5,000 visitors at the premiere of *Nowitzki. Der Perfekte Wurf.* 2,500 audience members in the cinema and 2,500 fans in front of the cinema. 100 journalists from all over the world. Dirk Nowitzki himself and his NBA team, the Dallas Mavericks, had traveled from Dallas in their private Boeing 757. I knew then that my biggest challenge would be to match the size of this premiere—the culmination of three years of work—with any of my later documentary movies.

TubeLounge: I reached my most recent milestone in 2016 when I started founding new companies with new business models, such as TubeLounge GmbH. It is based on setting up YouTube channels, around which we build social media communities. With Facebook, Twitter, Instagram, and Snapchat this is much easier than it was in 1999 with Nokia 9110s and 14k modems.

> What potential is hiding in people, products, and organizations that is still waiting to be discovered? Where are the potentials that aren't being used yet? And where do the strengths actually lie in totally different areas than we would have thought? Some people succeed in their endeavors without looking like they are even trying. Others fail at the simplest tasks because they misjudge themselves. Therefore, it is helpful to analyze one's strengths and weaknesses sensibly and deal with them honestly in order to identify and harness real potential.

Wladimir Klitschko is convinced:
If you keep an open mind, you will not just detect opportunities within yourself but also in others. This strengthens your understanding of people and sharpens your eye for aptitudes, talents, and opportunities.

"If We Leave Out the Unimportant, then the Important Will Become More Visible"

Project: To tell moving stories while producing commercially successful movies

Competitors/opponents: Film producers

Challenge: To identify the unimportant and to cut it out

When Broadview Pictures shot a movie documentary about Vitali and Wladimir Klitschko, a 10-strong film crew accompanied the brothers over a period of two years. They went to their childhood homes in Ukraine and Kazakhstan, came along to all boxing bouts during those two years, traveled to New York, Los Angeles, and Kiev, interviewed the coaches and filmed the brothers playing chess on vacation. They also documented the first time their mother and father talked about their sons publicly. The film crew was at every important press conference and caught on film the last few hours before a fight. They amassed endless amounts of material. The cutters then spent four and a half months in the cutting room, and the end product of all this was a movie that ran to four hours. To turn this into a movie of less than two hours which tells a moving and truthful story—that is the real art of film-making, from the point of view of the producers.

"The prerequisite for a good story is to research it conscientiously beforehand", Leopold Hoesch says. "The art of telling a true story in an exciting way is the art of leaving things out." Which characters and which plot shows potential? Which narrative strands are strong enough to make them into a gripping movie? What messages can they carry? "Kill your darlings" is what producers call the difficult step of getting rid of their favorite scenes.

The film became what is called a "coming of age" movie, lasting 110 minutes. It tells the story of how Vitali and Wladimir grew up and constantly spurred themselves and each other on. It shows how these icons and heroes of the masses celebrate together, how they share their suffering with each other after defeats, and how they changed the world of boxing through their presence as sports scientists educated to PhD level and as upstanding, fair personalities. Beyond boxing, the film also shows what it means to compete with each other and yet support and rely on each other. It shows what brothers can be for each other; and what it means not to find out who the stronger one is. *Klitschko* is the kind of movie you should watch with your brother.

Klitschko was nominated in New York for world-renowned "Sport Emmy" film prize, and won the famous "Romy Award" in Vienna. The movie was broadcast in almost every country in the world. Never before had the US American pay-TV channel HBO shown a movie in its original German and Russian with English subtitles.

That Vitali and Wladimir Klitschko had the potential to fill a whole movie does not come as a surprise given their level of fame. The matter of which topics and focal points would provide the best material for a documentary, however, only took shape slowly during the research period and during filming, Hoesch says.

It was clear from the start that the film was going to be a documentary. This is Hoesch's specialty and all of his films fall into this category. Yet even documentaries are subdivided into genres. Was it to be a crime story or a drama? A road movie or an adventure film? In theory, several types would have been possible options for the film about the Klitschkos, according to Hoesch. An action film for example—because of the setting in the world of boxing. Or a disaster movie because of the family's experiences during the Chernobyl disaster in 1986, which gets mentioned in passing. Hoesch saw the biggest potential in the story of brotherhood and of growing up into the two strongest men in the world.

The start of planning is also always the start of the challenge: How will the film-makers manage to move people with their subject matter? What needs to be shown and what left out? This question is already hanging in the air during pre-production, then during the shoot, and finally in post-production, during the cutting process. "Everything that gets shown needs to have meaning", Hoesch insists.

While they were researching, the director and the producer identified two strong plotlines:

On the one hand there were Wladimir Klitschko's sporting defeats in 2003 and 2004 and Vitali's "re-conquest" of the world champion's belt that Wladimir had lost. On the other hand there was the quarrel between the two men at that time. The film-makers decided on the plotline about the quarrel and from then on it was clear that this film was going to be a story about brothers.

As a result, many things just fell into place: Should for example Vitali's children be a theme in the film? No, because at that time they were of no importance for the plot. Why, however, did the parents get to have a say? Because it helps us understand the sons. When the mother explains that she has never seen any of her sons' fights because she is always beside herself with worry and just waits feverishly for the reassuring phone call after the fight to find out if her boys are okay, then this shows the audience the emotional state of the family.

Another example of Broadview TV's oeuvre is the film about Angela Merkel, which was shown in late 2016 on German television (on ARD and Arte) when the Chancellor announced that she was going to stand again in the next election. The potential of a documentary about the most powerful woman in the country is huge. Yet how does one tell a story about a woman like that, who is always in the public eye and about whom so much gets written and reported?

The Cinderella Story was the first working title of the film. "We wanted to show how a young girl from the northeastern province: who wasn't on anyone's radar, came to power", the producer recalls. "But during the development of the project we realized that this theory was not tenable. She was more Machiavelli than Cinderella." The next idea was entitled *Merkiavelli*—a nod to Niccolò Machiavelli's *The Prince*. Machiavelli's iconic work stands for the theory that the end justifies the means; that gaining and maintaining political power justifies use of any means, regardless of law and morality. "Yet this theory did not do Angela Merkel justice either," Hoesch says. In the end the film's title was *Angela Merkel. Die Unerwartete (The Unexpected)*. This title harbored the most potential both in his and the director's view: a woman who grew up a Protestant minister's daughter with humanist attitudes; a scientist who relies on data, not emotion; a woman who rose from the bottom right to the top without allowing herself to be manipulated.

Leopold Hoesch has now produced more than 150 films. In most of them he successfully lets the pictures tell the story, and sometimes he manages this without using the spoken word much at all. This wealth of experience helps him recognize and tell good stories, identify their potential, and harness it.

Nonetheless it is always a fresh challenge to unravel the subject matter to find out which might be the best possible plotline and then to develop this strand. "Every film is different", Leopold Hoesch stresses. "Only if we are prepared to combine structured processes with flexibility during production will we be able to achieve the best possible result: handcrafted unique works that have the potential to enthuse the masses in a different way." Fans would also add to this something that Hoesch did not make explicit: that he has an eye for gripping stories. It is the true stories of impressive people that give him the material which makes his movies stand out from the myriad documentaries that are released every year.

Identifying Potential and Harnessing It

Five Steps to Get to the Story with the Most Potential

1. **Relevance:** What is the story you want to tell? What message do you want to convey, what message has the potential to affect people's emotions? Make sure your story is relevant to your audience.

2. **Strong Personalities:** You need protagonists that are likeable even if they really are monsters. Attention: Be fair to the protagonists but do not go easy on them. You are not making your story for them but for the audience.

3. **Background:** You have to communicate. Insignificant details that do not add to the story (what we call "non-events") or even worse distract from it disturb the viewer on a conscious or subconscious level. Therefore anything that gets mentioned in your story should serve a purpose for the plotline.

4. **Story Arc:** All good stories have a narrative arc. A promising structure starts with an exposition and the introduction of the protagonist, leading towards the actual problem. After it has been made clear what the problem is (the "inciting incident"), you need to guide your protagonist through the difficulties of life. Near the end of the film comes the climax. During the climax, which mirrors the "inciting incident", the protagonist encounters in a dramatic way the solution and demise. Ideally you should stick to the criteria of the genre that you chose to establish in the introductory part of the film.

5. **The Art of Omission:** Your work is not yet done, once you have put everything together. This is the time to start getting rid of the ballast. Cut out anything that distracts from your core message. Be brave—"kill your darlings".

Top Performance

Mathias Ulmann, self-employed political and communications consultant, previously Group Creative Digital Strategist at DDB Germany, author of the book *Spin it! Denken und überzeugen wie ein Spin-Doktor (How to Think and Persuade like a Spin Doctor)*.

- Education: at the Institut d'Études Politiques de Paris (one of the Grandes Écoles), focusing on political and communication sciences

"Challenges are tests that are set for us by fate in order for us to develop and surpass ourselves. To master a challenge I always need other people. They help me understand all perspectives and levels."

Milestones

Fullsix France: At this marketing agency I held my first executive role as "Associate Creative Director". The agency had committed itself to digital topics and was growing at a time when the world of advertising was undergoing radical changes.

DDB Germany: This was my first position in Germany. I was the "Group Creative Digital Strategist" at the agency and dealt with consolidating digital thinking at all of the company's locations. In addition I also supported the CEO in the process of merging two subsidiaries into one group.

Parti Socialiste (PS) France: After working in the world of advertising I returned to my political roots. I worked as a speech writer and adviser for the party leader. It was a very intense time because I was accompanying and supporting a top politician during the period of François Hollande's presidency. This phase was marked by economic difficulties and national security problems.

> For top athletes this ability is essential: if you are at the top of your game in training, but cannot release the same level of performance in the real bout, you will never be a success. For businesses and executives, too, this ability is becoming increasingly important.

Wladimir Klitschko is convinced:
In times when business moves ever faster and becomes more and more complex, managers need to be able to pinpoint and access their knowledge and experiences at very short notice.

"Our Reaction Decides What Course a Crisis is Going to Take"

Project: Communication for a top politician: To filter true and relevant details from a wealth of information and to make them public within a short time frame

Competitors/Opponents: Opposition politicians, media, terrorists

Challenge: To control the story

It was nine o'clock on the morning of 7 January 2015 when two masked Al-Qaeda sympathizers attacked the offices of the satirical magazine *Charlie Hebdo* in Paris. Twelve people perished in the attack and several others were wounded. Less than four hours after this atrocity the communication chiefs of the leading politicians had already decided how to react to this monstrous act of terrorism: in a large-scale event they called on the people to gather all over France to demonstrate peacefully against Islamist terror and for French unity in the face of this attack. Four days later roughly four million people took to the streets in a number of cities around the country to march in remembrance of the victims. Among those present were foreign politicians such as the German chancellor Angela Merkel, the British prime minister at the time, David Cameron, and the Israeli prime minister Benjamin Netanyahu.

Mathias Ulmann was working for the chairman of the Parti Socialiste, Jean-Christophe Cambadélis, at that time. He wrote his speeches and statements, authored books, and organized the communication behind the scenes. Part of this was to accurately evaluate the power relationships in the system and to mobilize them for his goals. The *Charlie Hebdo* attack, although it was the first, was not the only attack during his time in French politics. It was, however, a pivotal experience. "From every catastrophe I learn something", he says. This sounds detached, yet it is the prerequisite for the Frenchman Ulmann's job: as a spin doctor he needs experience in both politics and communication. And he has to be able to suppress his emotions and to gain a clear overview even under the utmost pressure. This is the only way for him to be able to manage to access "frozen experience", as he calls it, at lightning speed; to explosively release top performance in order to find the best solutions.

Communications consultants like him have to keep calm even in the face of the most catastrophic events. And France in 2015 was subjected to a number of catastrophes, a whole series of attacks. Another tragic nadir was the attack on Paris bars, restaurants and the concert venue Bataclan, during which 130 people were massacred. Then, in the summer of 2016, 80 people were killed in Nice by a terrorist who drove his truck through crowds celebrating Bastille Day.

"The way you react decides what course the crisis is going to take", Ulmann says. He is aware of the power that words and visions have and he experiences every day that the way in which people view reality can be a key to success. He is proud of the restrained way in which the French political scene reacted after the first large attack, targeting the offices of *Charlie Hebdo*, and he is proud of the well-measured answer it found in the commemorative marches. Yet this is anything but easy: in volatile situations like these it is Ulmann's job to buy his employer time and space in which to think and act.

The start of such crisis communication is always signaled by his receiving an alarm by SMS. The Interior Ministry or the Ministry of Justice takes on the daily communication in the case of catastrophes. Behind the scenes there are dozens of advisers and spokespeople working away. To ensure that this works without a hitch, there are clear guidelines: Who talks to whom and in what order? Who has the authority to make decisions, and who is allowed to communicate them?

After an attack like that on *Charlie Hebdo* dozens of staff sift through the information. That in itself is a challenge because not all the information that is being circulated is true. It is also possible that the crisis is still actively ongoing. In the case of the *Charlie Hebdo* attack it took almost two days until the terrorists were caught. There is of course no way that those in charge can wait that long before informing the public. In such a case, therefore, the "frozen experience" comes into play, Ulmann says. In a crisis situation a multitude of decisions have to be made very quickly. The president, the prime minister, or other ministers are only confronted with the most important of these decisions, with all the rest being decided behind the scenes. For this, communication and exchanges among experienced colleagues are important, as is one's own capacity for abstract thought.

Once the actual facts of the situation have been established, it is up to experts like Ulmann to find the right words. In an hourly schedule he develops soundbites. His statements serve two functions: to inform and to introduce calm into the volatile public mood. "A president has to instill a sense of security in the face of terrible events like these. It is not his job to be emotional." If the President himself does not make a statement, there are six other politicians who are allowed to speak. No-one else.

Following the usual communication channels, information is disseminated to the public as well as to the administration and the political scene. In a pre-arranged order the communicators inform the party central office, active party members and other internal circles before the information is passed on to the national press agencies, the external and internal media as well as the social media teams. All of this happens in the space of just a few minutes.

Needless to say, communication goes both ways. The media call to ask questions, bloggers offer commentary, and the opposition parties issue statements. The spin doctor Ulmann has noticed that the higher the frequency of such catastrophic events is, the more brazen other parties' politicians become: In the case of *Charlie Hebdo* they held back critical comments about how the crisis had been dealt with for ten days, while after the Bataclan attack this was down to three days, and after the attack in Nice they issued critical comments immediately.

Furthermore, there are new enemies in addition to the old opponents, Ulmann says. These days even terrorists have professional means of communication, and the political scene still needs fully to adapt to this. There is, however, one significant difference: "We are permanently on guard. We have structures in place that enable us to go into crisis mode immediately."

The thing that makes Mathias Ulmann's job so challenging and, in his view, so exciting is that crises and the political language necessitated by them form the basis of politics. The multitude of events that happened in short succession demonstrates this. In just three months between late 2016 and early 2017 all of the following events took place: Donald Trump was sworn in as US president. François Hollande was not in a position to seek re-election as French president. Hollande's predecessor Nicolas Sarkozy lost in the primaries. There were also two government reshuffles, and a number of terrorist attacks and attempted attacks. All of these are situations during which a client needs quick reactions, self-control, inventiveness, team spirit and quick-wittedness, but mainly the right approach by the spin doctors.

And the spin doctors know all too well: In the world of today's media there is no way of controlling communication. Even the best script or the popular story-telling is useless. "On our digitalized and fast-moving stage, even the most detailed and tightly structured narrative cannot survive the first minute of its reading in a digital setting. This is something we need to work with."

Releasing Top Performance Explosively

Work Like a Spin Doctor

1. Where am I? Pinpoint your exact position in the implicit organization chart of power and respect it. It is important that you know who sits at the top and who at the bottom so that you can handle their differing states of mind and act in a goal-oriented way. Beware of people who stress that they are not interested in playing political power games. It is just these people who pursue their micropolitical tactics cunningly but hidden under the surface.

2. First Comes the Clan, then Comes the Plan: You need a loyal and reliable core team. Always communicate internally first, and then step by step externally. Even though you might have the best ideas, they will be utterly in vain if you lack allies to cover your back.

3. Zooming in, zooming out: Think in broad terms and then zoom in on the topics in questions. Create a permanent balance between breadth and depth. In a crisis situation I throw all my knowledge at the problem and completely banish insignificant things from my thoughts in order to work explosively.

4. "Not now": Debriefing does not happen on the battlefield. Only after the battle has been fought do you have time to debrief. Mistakes will happen anyway. Nonetheless, onwards and upwards. The team is not there to be perfect but to improve the situation and the outlook permanently.

5. After the crisis is before the next crisis: Tap into the knowledge and experience of the veterans of your sector. From them you can learn all those things that active spin doctors are not willing to share with you. Read as much as you can and do not omit the Social Sciences. You will get through the next crisis by drawing on your accurate and "frozen", meaning retrievable, knowledge as well as by means of your "cultural charisma".

Way 11
Organizational Structures

Astrid Schulte, managing director of bellybutton International GmbH, CMO at Kanz Financial Holding (KFH) as well as member of the management board of Kids Brands House N.V.; previous positions include marketing director at Cartier Northern Europe and director of Loyalty Partner GmbH (payback)

- Education: Business Administration at the ESB Business School in Reutlingen/Reims

"Challenge to me means growing steadily myself and supporting the people around me in their own growth while always remaining myself and staying true to myself."

Milestones

Kraft Foods Group: This position was my first job after I finished my degree. As a brand manager I learnt structured thinking and analyzing figures. I also found out that in corporations a lot of time is spent on "politics".

Roland Berger Strategy Consultants: "Anything is possible" is what I learnt as a corporate consultant: sleeping little, learning a lot in a short time, being able to solve any challenge. This realization set me free and relieved my fear.

Loyalty Partner ("payback"): "Thinking big" really does make you big! As the director for marketing and sales I visited the boardrooms of all major German companies to acquire new customers. I saw how companies are built: with dedication, a clear strategy, and the unshakeable belief that you can do it.

> In a small team it can be difficult to introduce clear structures and clearly assign responsibilities because the staffing level is so low. Similarly in large companies there is a danger that such clearly assigned responsibilities and hierarchies might smother their employees' empowerment.

Wladimir Klitschko is convinced:
That is why it is important to create structures that turn the company into an empowered organization. Everyone should be given the space to develop their commitment and self-reliance without, however, relegating the idea of team responsibility and individual responsibility to the background.

"Flexibility Is an Important Structural Element"

Project: Establishing bellybutton, selling it to a strategic investor, integrating the brand into the company

Competitors/Opponents: Babies' and children's clothing companies

Challenge: To build a brand from scratch with a clear internal and external vision. Later on, to draw synergies from the merger with a strategic investor while maintaining the culture of the different units

When Astrid Schulte sold the majority of bellybutton to a strategic investor in early 2014, this led to big changes for the Hamburg-based supplier of maternity wear and children's and baby clothes. Kids Fashion Group is a holding company comprising 16 children's fashion brands, whose ranks bellybutton joined. Since then, the bellybutton brand has been marketed by 40 sales representatives instead of one, and it gets presented in eight showrooms rather than just one. However, for the original staff it was not all positives. Instead of about 40 staff, today bellybutton directly employs only 20. Many aspects are covered by the shared service center of the holding.

Yet this is exactly what Astrid Schulte's goal was: she wanted bellybutton to grow and for that she needed a strong partner. Now it was up to her to create suitable organizational structures while ensuring that the company culture did not suffer.

"Structures always reflect a culture and an idea of humanity," Astrid Schulte is sure. At bellybutton she had succeeded in creating a kind of cult and through this a very special culture. The company did not just try to sell products but also to create a living environment and a shared belief. Bellybutton had been founded in 1997 by four women because they were unhappy with the product range on offer for pregnant women. These four friends, among them the actress Ursula Karven and the former model Dana Schweiger, started out with cosmetics and later widened their product range to include fashionable maternity wear as well as contemporary baby and children's clothes. Astrid Schulte joined them in 2001 as managing director and proved to be a good addition, not just because of her background in marketing and sales. During her first years with the company she was "pregnant almost all the time," she says with a grin, and as a mother of three served as a good role model for their brand.

bellybutton's new interpretation of being pregnant appealed to the target group, and this positive feeling was also reflected among staff. "I was looking for people who were on the same wavelength as us proprietors," Schulte explains, people who were interested in the subject matter and who showed commitment, meaning dedication and passion. The company culture has always been characterized by a high degree of openness, a lot of dedication to the firm's success, and the conviction that finding a balance in life makes everyone happier and better, the managing director says. The staff joining bellybutton particularly appreciated the compatibility between their job and their family life. bellybutton has always employed a lot of mothers.

This flexibility made its mark on the start-up in every respect and defined the way people worked together. The company was carried along by shared values. In the beginning, as Astrid Schulte recalls, there was no explicit structure. Although each member of staff was hired for a particular area of responsibility, they all had to be prepared to work in other areas nonetheless.

At one point the accounts department was experiencing IT problems. As a result, all staff pitched in, wrote invoices and demands for payment and generally helped wherever help was needed. In a similar vein it was common practice for projects to be run and taken responsibility for on a broader basis than the concrete responsibilities. That the staff were happy with this way of organizing work is evident from the extremely low staff turnover. Over the first ten years it was below 5 percent each year.

The "why" was clear to everyone, Schulte says. "We wanted bellybutton to be increasingly successful and increasing numbers of women to be able to share the brand's attitude to life." Namely that life with children is fulfilling. That every woman will find her own role in her new life as a mother through strength and self-confidence. And that mothers do not have to be perfect.

In 2012 the time had come for Schulte to accelerate the firm's growth further. The company's sales volume amounted to approximately 20 million euros at that time. As the company's director, Schulte went on a customer acquisition tour for two months and returned to Hamburg having secured contracts with two major clients. While she was satisfied with having won the major players in the children's clothing market as distribution partners, this step also marked a turning point for her company. bellybutton had to create new structures. Up until then, its customers had been specialist shops and boutiques, but now it had to be able to supply large department stores. For this it needed investment. The company bought in a merchandise management system that enabled the department stores to check with a simple mouse click what products were available. The cost of the necessary broadband connection alone amounted to a six-figure sum. At the same time bellybutton had to deal with the new issue of "visual merchandising": The major customers felt that they should not be held responsible for maintaining the retail space dedicated to bellybutton products, but that this ought to be done by the company itself. This led to a situation where employees from accounts or purchasing were taking turns to spend a week each going round the department stores to service the retail areas there.

"This was not a long-term solution," Schulte admits. "We needed more manpower and more financial scope." In the end, they set out in search of an investor and came to an agreement with the Kids Fashion Group (KFG) based in Pliezhausen in Baden-Württemberg in southern Germany. This company already comprised children's fashion brands such as Kanz, Königsmühle, Marc O'Polo Junior as well as Steiff Collection, and it was perfectly set up for supplying large distribution partners. And even better: KFH had its own production sites, for example in Turkey, which would enable bellybutton to offer their products very soon after at significantly lower prices. While the purchasing and sales departments moved wholesale to Pliezhausen, Schulte and her Hamburg-based staff have since been dealing with the licensing business, the marketing, and the online business for all KFH brands.

bellybutton maintained flexibility as a structural element, Schulte emphasizes. She considers a certain "we'll get to grips with this topic" mentality important because an organization, no matter how well-structured it is, has to be able to think quickly, activate knowledge and react. As a member of the board of the stock corporation Kids Brands House, Astrid Schulte did not just gain responsibility, she also had to relinquish some. She is sharing the management of bellybutton with two managers from KFG.

What mattered to the businesswoman Schulte was that the result was a win-win situation: "We benefit from the group's know-how, and they benefit from bellybutton's culture."

Creating Organizational Structures

Five Steps towards an Effective, Agile Organization

1. **Answer the Question of Why:** More important than "what a company does and how" is the question of what the superordinate guiding idea is. First put a mission statement into words as this will give everyone in the team a guideline for how to act and simultaneously instill in them the feeling of being a part of something big. Decisions are made more easily and effectively when the common mission statement provides clarity for everyone.

2. **Self-organization instead of Dominance:** It is not the executives who give out tasks or define goals. Instead, alternating team members are asked to take the lead on projects. The traditional job description of the executive role is changing and is being geared towards enabling and empowering the staff. If the structure in your organization so far has been pyramid-shaped then you need to start leading your employees towards an agile working method in small steps. The best way is to start with whichever department seems to you most open to changes.

3. **Turning Shared Values into a Corporate Culture:** Shared values are the basis for working together as well as the driver of the business. Work out what it is that characterizes your company. Dedication and feedback could be among the values, just like courage, openness or tolerance. Heterogeneous cultures, which enable everyone to be themselves, produce the best results. Because then employees can be authentic and do not have to pretend. If individual members of the team do not live by these values, it is up to their colleagues to address it with them.

4. **Working Methods:** Effectiveness rather than perfectionism! If you use agile working methods, drafts are being opened up to discussion already at a very early stage. It is no longer about an individual person's ingenious

ideas, but about incorporating as much input as possible. Feedback is essential, and visualization techniques become increasingly important. Lengthy planning cycles however are now obsolete. Establish a culture that embraces open discussion and feedback.

5. Direct and Fast Communication: Quick communication without organizational barriers is indispensable for an effective organization. The goals, actions and the roles of the individuals have to be clear and get adjusted regularly. For example you could introduce "daily standup meetings": short morning meetings held while standing up. Every individual informs the others about the state of his or her project, questions are discussed and new work parcels handed out. This should last no longer than 15 minutes.

Strengths and Weaknesses

Torsten Bittlingmaier, personnel expert, founder of TalentManagers

- Most recently CEO of Haufe Akademie, previously head of corporate talent management at Deutsche Telekom AG
- Education: Business Studies at Berufsakademie Mannheim, Germany

"Challenges are tasks that I cannot solve off the top of my head. They force me out of my comfort zone and are usually uncomfortable. If I master them, however, I progress in my development. By the end I always have a smile on my face."

Milestones

ABB Mannheim: Human resources was something that I had found boring while I was studying. I specialized in IT and organizational matters, but at ABB I had the opportunity to learn HR from scratch after all. That's when I found it was exactly the right job for me.

MAN Nutzfahrzeuge (now MAN Truck and Bus): I was given my first big executive position. MAN was just emerging from a crisis and slowly beginning to become successful again. In this situation I was able, as Head of HR and Organizational Development, to re-think all topics using a greenfield approach. That was both exciting and challenging. At that time I was the only executive in MAN's HR sector without legal training. The whole HR team in the company was characterized by their administrative and juridical approach. This meant that I had a great deal of convincing to do at several levels.

Deutsche Telekom: What a corporation: a supertanker of a company with 250,000 employees. These are dimensions that I had not worked with before then. I was in charge of Talent Management and found it very challenging to kick off initiatives that actually had an impact.

Deutsche Telekom was a valuable learning experience because the working conditions were unique: politics exerts an influence on its business model; it is part-owned by the state; some employees are covered by the collective bargaining law, others by the civil service law... From an HR manager's point of view it presents the largest possible challenge.

> In the world of work there are few people who are as tuned into analyzing their opponents as athletes. If they did not evaluate their opponent's strengths and weaknesses, they might as well just not turn up to the competition at all.

Wladimir Klitschko is convinced:
Executives can also benefit from this. Because if you know your competitors and their pros and cons, then you will be much better prepared for competing for the same customers as them.

"If I Know the Others' Weaknesses I Can Use It for My Own Purposes"

Business Idea: Support, talent consulting and finding jobs for executives and specialists at their request ("reverse headhunting")

Opponents: Headhunters, recruitment consultants, coaches, lawyers

Challenge: Making use of the weaknesses of other players on the market; cooperating with them while fully making the most of one's own strengths.

How do applicants usually come across suitable job vacancies? Mostly, employers advertise their open positions, sift through the applications, invite promising talents for an interview, and decide which applicant appears to be the best. Often they are supported in this process by recruitment consultants. If the search is particularly difficult or delicate, they may use a headhunter to search for, present and recommend applicants at the company's request. This is the way firms have been operating for decades.

Recently the search for specialists and executives has been getting more difficult. Employers have a smaller pool of talent to choose from. They are struggling to attract enough suitable applicants—for financial and IT positions for example. Whilst for decades it was the employers who had the most clout and were able to select their preferred candidates from a wealth of applicants, nowadays it is well-qualified workers who can pick the most attractive job offer from several offers received. The job market is changing: from an employers' market to a job seekers' market.

This development is something that Torsten Bittlingmaier has been paying close attention to as an HR manager. For more than twenty years he has been able to analyze the strengths and weaknesses of the market players. He noticed how the entire market was being transformed. He also saw headhunters and recruitment consultants getting under pressure because recruiting managers have long since started searching the internet themselves to find candidates and to approach them directly. Business networks such as LinkedIn or XING have made it easy for them to do this.

If you wanted to paint a bleak picture you might go as far as predicting the demise of the profession of recruitment service providers as a whole. Yet the developments do not bear this out and probably never will because there will always be companies that cannot cope with mastering the search process by themselves; because there will always be hard-to-fill positions for which employers need help; and because some employers simply have such a high demand that they need to outsource their recruiting due to their own lack of capacity.

Nonetheless we can agree on one thing: If the job market is changing from an employers' to a job seekers' market, then it will be a weakness in the recruitment consultants' and headhunters' business model if they stick with the idea of companies being their sole clients.

Because the (financial) pressures on their businesses are rising, they have hardly any time left to proactively get to know new candidates and add them to their database. Instead, they are busy trying to work through the search requests by companies in the most efficient way possible.

Their strength in the midst of this transformation lies in their excellent contacts with companies, HR departments and top management.

Torsten Bittlingmaier therefore founded a business that makes the most of the way the market is developing and of the strengths and weaknesses of the market players. His start-up TalentManagers, which he set up in 2015, specializes in services for highly qualified candidates: advising them, aiding their professional development, and recommending them to suitable employers. "Reverse headhunting", in other words. Just like professional sportspeople or artists have their own manager, top managers and specialists will in the future also have a careers manager at their side, of this Bittlingmaier is convinced.

The services that talent managers offer are as follows: They work out tangible career goals and next steps with the candidates, bring them together with potential employers, place them, support them during contract negotiations and also provide help later on during salary negotiations or possible severance agreements. Alternatively, they can just make sure that there is a plan B, even though currently there may be no need for change. In the long term, Bittlingmaier thinks, it might even be possible for talent managers to take on negotiating contracts with the HR department on behalf of their clients.

As always when a totally new business idea is born, it will take a while to establish itself. Bittlingmaier, however, has already got his hands full just a short time after setting up his firm. Just by word of mouth he is already at the peak of his capacity. As a consequence he has decided to find further partners to enable TalentManagers to expand.

Instead of abusing the weakness of recruitment consultants and thus risking a major confrontation with their large, establish and well-organized profession, Bittlingmaier draws on their might and cooperates with them. While he sees his own role as that of a sparring partner for the candidates, the recruitment consultants and headhunters provide services for the employers. Bittlingmaier requires open positions to place his candidates. The recruitment consultants, on the other hand, require candidates who they can suggest to their clients. It is a win-win situation for both parties.

So far this kind of cooperation is loose and on demand. If TalentManagers is searching for a challenge for one of its candidates, Bittlingmaier phones recruitment consultants he knows. They, in turn, call him if they have a vacancy to fill for which they have not managed to find a suitable candidate.

If candidate and vacancy are a good match, Bittlingmaier supports his client through the rest of the process: What strengths have they got that makes them the perfect person for the job? What positives have they got to offer that other applicants may not have? And are there any personal contacts in the target company who may be helpful during the application process or the placement by a headhunter, as the case may be?

During this process, Bittlingmaier again uses the same philosophy as in his demarcation from the headhunters: He solves the challenge by making the most of his own strengths, or those of the candidate, and using the weaknesses of others. This even impacts the revenue model of TalentManagers: His clients pay a modest annual fee to use the services of the start-up. Bittlingmaier deliberately kept the fees low in order to minimize the entry threshold and to attract for example newly qualified professionals. His actual income is generated by means of a commission charged on successful placements.

If over the course of the months he manages to place his client in a company—regardless of whether by using a recruitment consultant or his own contacts—he receives a one-off payment of an agreed percentage of the candidate's new annual salary. There have even been a few occasions already where the new employer has offered to cover this commission fee. Because in relation to the cost of a headhunter—who would usually demand a third of the annual salary—it is comparatively low. Also, the company can be assured that it has found in this new starter the best possible candidate. This is because, with the support of and professional development by the talent manager, the candidate proactively and whole-heartedly decided in favor of this position.

Knowing and Using Your Opponent's Strengths and Weaknesses

Applying the Method to Setting Up a Business

1. Already while Drawing up the Start-up Idea and Market Analysis, the Central Question Is: What strengths and—even more importantly—what weaknesses do the competitors and the other market players have? Who are your customers actually going to be?

2. What State Is the Market in? Is it saturated? Is it undergoing a transformation? Does this open up opportunities for newcomers that established companies have not got?

3. Is Speed a Factor During Market Entry in Order to Be Able to Use this Opportunity? If so, do not resort to frenzied activity. Take the time to understand the customers' needs and to base your idea on them.

4. Play to Your Strengths, whether They Be a Different Market Entry, a Technological Advantage, More Service or Bespoke Provision. Align your offer accordingly.

5. Is There the Possibility for a Win-Win Situation? Which market player might be a suitable partner because you can compensate for their weaknesses with your strengths? (See also Way 1: Coopetition)

Epilogue

Don't Listen to the Naysayers!

When I think of Wladimir Klitschko, I do so as both a friend and a fan. Wladimir is one of the most extraordinary and outstanding fighters I have ever experienced. He reminds me of an ancient Greek god: the expressiveness of his face, the broad shoulders, the athletic, V-shaped small of his back. Every part of his body is defined by muscle. There he stands, upright in the ring, looking his opponent straight in the eyes and getting ready to land the knockout blow.

Yet it is not just his physical qualities that make Wladimir strong. Wladimir has the right mentality—this is what makes him a magnificent fighter. He has been hungry for the next big goal all his life. This surely has something to do with how he grew up. He came from a modest background and grew up in the system of the former Soviet Union. To get out of there and travel the world was an additional motivating factor for him. Early on, he threw himself into the world of boxing, knowing full well that there was no alternative for him. Soon he had a very precise vision of wanting to become an Olympic winner.

I know what it's like when you want to get away from your home, from your old life. I myself grew up under difficult circumstances in a small village in Austria. It was the thought of making it that motivated me. I wanted to achieve great things and avoid at any cost returning to my boring life.

People like Wladimir or myself or, for example, Muhammad Ali are united by a special ambition, an incredible power of will which stems from our origins. We were sure that there was a bigger world waiting for us out there. I still remember the first time I saw a documentary about America: the huge skyscrapers, the shiny cars. I knew immediately: That's where I want to go!

Nonetheless, it was anything but easy for me when I emigrated to the USA in 1968—to a totally strange country. I did not speak the language and had neither money nor friends. All I had was my bodybuilding title of "Mister Universe", my willpower and my ambition. There just is no simple way to the top. In life there will always be challenges, but you can deal with them and overcome them. Over time I learnt to fight hard. The bigger the goal, the bigger the obstacles. If I choose an easy-to-reach goal then I won't run into too many problems on the way there. To tackle for example Mount Everest, however, is dangerous and time-consuming. The same is true for Wladimir, who first aimed to win the Olympic Games and then to become boxing world champion. That is nothing for weak personalities, only for someone strong.

This strength of Wladimir's comes from his mother, who has played a huge role in his life. I spent some time with them both when I visited Wladimir at his training camp in Kitzbühel in Austria. I found the relationship between the two of them really moving: the affectionate way he speaks to her and the incredible love you can see in his eyes. His mother supports, encourages and believes in him. She taught him how he can master even difficult tasks—if he throws his willpower behind it. Winning is not always important in this; fun and optimism are what matters.

In fact, the feeling of failure is part of a top athlete's life. Without ever failing you will never become one of the greats, this is what athletes learn right from the start. The definition of a winner is always to get back up, no matter what happened. Only losers stay on the floor.

Wladimir is just such a winner: He too failed and lost some fights. Yet he always boxed his way back up and never lost his positive mindset. What I admire in Wladimir is that he learns more from his mistakes than from his successes. This attitude is one of his biggest strengths. I am certain that Wladimir will succeed in using this ability after his sporting career is over. He cannot keep boxing forever. There will come a time when he has to stop. He will always be good at what he does, whatever it may be. Whether it is his family, his foundation or his business—he approaches them all in the same way. What he learnt in his sport helps him in his second career. I am looking forward to seeing what he is going to do with his talents in the future, what he is going to pass on.

For me too, in my career as a bodybuilder, there came a point when I had to stop. I frequently sustained injuries and took longer to recover. After my time as an actor I went into politics. To become Governor of California in 2003 was the biggest challenge of my life. It was such a big thing for me to be allowed to spend eight years representing nearly 40 million people and the eighth largest economy in the world. It was the single largest honor I was ever granted in my life. When I decided to become a politician, everyone around me thought that was impossible. All my life people have been telling me: You won't manage that. That's too big for you. You are mad. I think this is what happens when you dream big. But I always followed Nelson Mandela on this:

"It always seems impossible until it's done."

Wladimir made similar experiences in his life and his sporting career. He was often surrounded by negative voices—people who did not believe in him. But he was clever enough not to listen to these naysayers. He always knew exactly what his vision was. And it will be the same in the future.

Arnold Schwarzenegger

Acknowledgments

All the people I met along my way have made me what I am today. Without exception.

Needless to say my parents are the foundations: Wladimir and Nadia, whom I admire and love endlessly.

Over the first 14 years of my life they instilled strong values in me until I left the family home. From the moment I was born until the age of three I was treated like an angel, from three to fourteen like a slave, and from fourteen onwards like a friend.

I count myself lucky that I had a constant companion—both mentally and physically. He is my unique and best friend, my mother, father, adviser, motivator and never-tiring challenger: my beloved brother Vitali.

My family has grown over time. They help me take on every single challenge in line with our shared values. I want to thank them for that.

Index